JUSTICE
IN OUR TIME

THE JAPANESE CANADIAN REDRESS

SETTLEMENT

JUSTICE
IN OUR TIME

THE JAPANESE CANADIAN REDRESS SETTLEMENT

ROY MIKI AND CASSANDRA KOBAYASHI

Preface by Art Miki

Talonbooks
Vancouver

**National Association of
Japanese Canadians**
Winnipeg

1991

copyright © 1991 National Association of Japanese Canadians

Published with the assistance of the Canada Council and the Japanese Canadian Redress Foundation.

Talonbooks
201/1019 Cordova Street
Vancouver, British Columbia
Canada V6A 1M8

National Association of Japanese Canadians
782 Corydon Avenue
Winnipeg, Manitoba
Canada R3M 0Y1

Designed by Seabrook & Bobolo Limited using QuarkXPress 3.0
Typefaces: Garamond and 55 Helvetica
Printed and bound in Canada by Hignell Printing Ltd.
First printing: August, 1991.

Canadian Cataloguing in Publication Data

Miki, Roy, 1942-
    Justice in our time

    Co-published by the National Association of Japanese Canadians.
    ISBN 0-88922-292-4 (Talonbooks). — ISBN 0-9694756-1-6 (NAJC)

    1. Japanese-Canadians — Evacuation and relocation, 1942-1945.
2. World War, 1939-1945 — Reparations. I. Kobayashi, Cassandra, 1952- II.
National Associations of Japanese Canadians. III. Title.
FC106.J3M54 1991   971'.004956   C91-091500-8   F1035.J3M54 1991

TABLE OF CONTENTS

ACKNOWLEDGEMENT

As a people, Canadians commit themselves to the creation of a society that ensures equality and justice for all, regardless of race or ethnic origin.

During and after World War II, Canadians of Japanese ancestry, the majority of whom were citizens, suffered unprecedented actions taken by the Government of Canada against their community.

Despite perceived military necessities at the time, the forced removal and internment of Japanese Canadians during World War II and their deportation and expulsion following the war, was unjust. In retrospect, government policies of disenfranchisement, detention, confiscation and sale of private and community property, expulsion, deportation and restriction of movement, which continued after the war, were influenced by discriminatory attitudes. Japanese Canadians who were interned had their property liquidated and the proceeds of sale were used to pay for their own internment.

The acknowledgement of these injustices serves notice to all Canadians that the excesses of the past are condemned and that the principles of justice and equality in Canada are reaffirmed.

Therefore, the Government of Canada, on behalf of all Canadians, does hereby:

1) acknowledge that the treatment of Japanese Canadians during and after World War II was unjust and violated principles of human rights as they are understood today;

2) pledge to ensure, to the full extent that its powers allow, that such events will not happen again; and

3) recognize, with great respect, the fortitude and determination of Japanese Canadians who, despite great stress and hardship, retain their commitment and loyalty to Canada and contribute so richly to the development of the Canadian nation.

RECONNAISSANCE

En tant que nation, les Canadiens se sont engagés à édifier une société qui respecte les principes d'égalité et de justice pour tous ses membres sans égard à leurs origines culturelles ou raciales.

Pendant et après la Deuxième Guerre mondiale, des Canadiens d'origine japonaise, citoyens de notre pays pour la plupart, ont eu à souffrir de mesures sans précédent prises par le gouvernement du Canada et dirigées contre leur communauté.

En dépit des besoins militaires perçus à l'époque, le déplacement forcé et l'internement de Canadiens japonais au cours de la Deuxième Guerre mondiale, ainsi que leur déportation et leur expulsion au lendemain de celle-ci, étaient injustifiables. On se rend compte aujourd'hui que les mesures gouvernementales de privation des droits civiques, de détention, de confiscation et de vente des biens personnels et communautaires, ainsi que d'expulsion, de déportation et de restriction des déplacements, qui ont été maintenues après la guerre, découlaient d'attitudes discriminatoires. Les Canadiens japonais internés ont vu leurs biens liquidés, le produit de la vente de ceux-ci servant à payer leur propre internement.

En reconnaissant ces injustices, nous voulons signifier à tous les Canadiens que nous condamnons les abus commis dans le passé et que nous reconfirmons pour le Canada les principes de justice et d'égalité.

En conséquence, le gouvernement du Canada, au nom de tous les Canadiens :

1) reconnaît que les mesures prises à l'encontre des Canadiens japonais pendant et après la Deuxième Guerre mondiale étaient injustes et constituaient une violation des principes des droits de la personne, tels qu'ils sont compris aujourd'hui;

2) s'engage à faire tout en son pouvoir pour que de tels agissements ne se reproduisent plus jamais;

3) salue, avec grand respect, la force d'âme et la détermination des Canadiens japonais qui, en dépit d'épreuves et de souffrances considérables, ont conservé envers le Canada leur dévouement et leur loyauté, contribuant grandement à l'épanouissement de la nation canadienne.

Prime Minister of Canada   Le Premier ministre du Canada

PREFACE

by ART MIKI *President, National Association of Japanese Canadians*

September 22, 1988 is a day that I will always remember. I sat in the House of Commons and heard the words of Prime Minister Brian Mulroney, addressed to the Japanese Canadian community for the injustices they suffered during and after World War II:

> Mr. Speaker, I know I speak for members of all sides of the House in offering to Japanese Canadians the formal and sincere apology of this Parliament for those past injustices against them, their families, and their heritage, and our solemn commitment to Canadians of every origin that they will never again be countenanced or repeated.

As I listened to the carefully chosen words of the Prime Minister's speech announcing the Redress Agreement negotiated with the National Association of Japanese Canadians (NAJC), memories of the five years of the redress campaign flashed through my mind—the struggle within the Japanese Canadian community, the struggle with the Government and five successive Ministers of State for Multiculturalism, and the struggle to win the approval of the Canadian public. The redress issue became a test for all of us who were involved in the NAJC. Would we be able to take and maintain a strong position on redress, and would we be able to persist until our goal of a "just and honourable" settlement was achieved?

NAJC President Art Miki and his family, uprooted from Haney, BC, ended up in Ste. Agathe, Manitoba, a small French Canadian town. Clockwise, from lower right: Art Miki, age 5; his younger brother Les Miki, age 4; his grandfather Tokusaburo Ooto; his father Kazuo Miki; his uncle Tak Ooto; family friends Kunesaburo *Hayakawa and Nori Hayakawa; his grandmother Yoshi Ooto. Absent from the photo are his sister Joan, age 2, and his mother, Shizuko (Ooto) Miki, who was pregnant with his brother Roy.* Courtesy of Shizuko Miki.

It was in January 1984, at a meeting in Winnipeg, that the NAJC Council officially resolved to seek an acknowledgement of the injustices endured by Japanese Canadians during and after the Second World War, financial compensation for the injustices, and a review and amendment of the War Measures Act and relevant sections of the Charter of Rights and Freedoms so that no Canadian would ever again be subject to such wrongs. The decision to undertake a redress movement was a bold step for a community small

sions had to be overcome before we could establish a meaningful process of dialogue and debate within the national Japanese Canadian community, but once the NAJC Council began to develop a campaign to reach a community consensus for a settlement package, the grassroots Japanese Canadian community was drawn into the redress movement.

The process of seeking redress became a profound learning experience for all of us. We had to devise campaign strategies as we proceeded, and often we were faced with complicated decisions that had to be made under pressure. As I look back over the years of struggle, from 1984 to 1988, several critical landmarks remain. The NAJC's brief, *Democracy Betrayed*, made public on November 21, 1984, was the first occasion on which the Japanese Canadian community voiced its call for a just and honourable resolution to the injustices of the 1940s. Then came the Price Waterhouse report, *Economic Losses to Japanese Canadians After 1941*, completed in May 1986, the first documented study of the material losses to Japanese Canadians resulting from the wartime uprooting. While research for the report was being done, the NAJC held many community meetings on redress across the country to determine a community position, and in the spring of 1986, the NAJC polled Japanese Canadians on the content of a settlement package. That period of the campaign culminated in May 1986 with a meeting in Winnipeg where the NAJC Council announced a comprehensive redress proposal, the components of which were eventually included in the Redress Agreement signed with the Government on September 22, 1988.

The most gratifying experience of the redress movement was the genuine interest and involvement of those Japanese Canadians who

in number and lacking the necessary political knowledge and influence.

I was elected president of the NAJC at that meeting in Winnipeg. Little did I realize that during the early period of my presidency I would be quickly initiated into the fermenting political turmoil within the NAJC itself. There were several people vying for control over the direction of the redress movement and they used procedural roadblocks wherever possible to disrupt the NAJC's fledgling campaign. These internal divi-

took up the challenge and succeeded. What began as a "voice in the wilderness" became a Canadian issue of national prominence. The earlier cynicism of many Japanese Canadians gradually gave way to a belief that redress might be possible in their lifetime. Such a change in attitudes was heartening, but it did not occur without a lot of hard work by many committed people. I think of Japanese Canadian seniors, like Norman Oikawa of Hamilton and George Kakuno of Kelowna, both now deceased, who played a vital role in keeping the flame of redress alive, even when it may have appeared an almost hopeless task.

Alongside those Japanese Canadians who supported the NAJC, sometimes despite antagonistic reactions from friends, family and their community, there were Canadians from all walks of life who joined the National Coalition for Japanese Canadian Redress to call for a just and honourable settlement. Many organizations representing unions, churches, ethnic, multicultural and civil liberties groups wrote letters supporting the NAJC to the Prime Minister and participated at rallies and meetings. Certain politicians, especially the multicultural critics, Sergio Marchi of the Liberal Party and Ernie Epp of the New Democratic Party (NDP), consistently raised the redress issue in the House of Commons during Question Period and arranged for the NAJC Strategy Committee to meet with their leaders, John Turner of the Liberal Party and Ed Broadbent of the NDP, during the critical periods of the campaign.

For me the high point in the redress movement came at the Redress Forum in Ottawa, in April 1988. The National Coalition for Japanese Canadian Redress, a powerful group of individuals and organizations from all over Canada, was represented there, and was joined by hundreds of Japanese Canadian seniors from all over Canada. That event received considerable media coverage and effectively confirmed that the political process could be influenced. Soon after, the NAJC opened discussions with the Honourable Gerry Weiner. Previous Ministers of State for Multiculturalism had failed to resolve the issue of redress with the NAJC. It is to the credit of Gerry Weiner, with the personal support of Lucien Bouchard, then Secretary of State, that the Conservative government of Prime Minister Brian Mulroney negotiated a settlement with the NAJC.

Justice in Our Time celebrates the redress settlement achieved by the NAJC. The chronological documentation of the NAJC's campaign, from its beginnings to its resolution on September 22, 1988, recounts the story of the political struggle of Japanese Canadians to break the silence of their past and to seek justice in our time. Redress was a complex issue that reverberated in every nook and cranny of my community, and it was a volatile issue that, at times, threatened to divide us. In the process, though, it was a liberating issue that brought us together in our desire to reach a meaningful settlement. I hope that our story will remain, for future generations of Canadians, a prime example of one community's struggle to overcome the devastating effects of racism, and to affirm the rights of all individuals in a democracy.

Art Miki and Prime Minister Brian Mulroney on signing the historic Redress Agreement in the Parliament Building on September 22, 1988. Miki became a Member of the Order of Canada in 1991.
Photo: Gordon King.

12

> *" Tears of happiness fell. "*
>
> *Mrs. Tsune Ochiai, 92, from "40 Years of Waiting Over for Montreal Family," Barbara Newborn,* The Senior Times *(Montreal), October 1988.*

HISTORICAL BACKGROUND

THE VIOLATION OF CITIZENSHIP RIGHTS

In the spring of 1941, before the war broke out, the Royal Canadian Mounted Police (RCMP) fingerprinted and registered all Japanese Canadians over the age of 16. They were required to carry with them an identification card until 1949. This card for nisei Yosh Arai is reproduced from Justice in Our Time *(NAJC, 1988). Courtesy of Yosh Arai.*

The Bearer, whose photograph and specimen of signature appear hereon, has been duly registered in compliance with the provisions of Order-in-Council P. C. 117.

Registered by Custodian

Vancouver (Date) March 31st, 1941.

CANADIAN BORN

Issuing Officer _____ INSPECTOR C.M.P.

> "*I remember my dad talking about British justice and fair play. He really believed they'd never do it to us because we were Canadian. He was proved wrong within weeks.*"
>
> *Yosh Arai, quoted in "Federal Offices Now Occupy Spot Taken from Japanese-Canadian," by Nancy Knickerbocker,* Vancouver Sun, *May 31, 1986.*

In 1942, on the west coast of British Columbia, some 22,000 men, women and children of Japanese ancestry—75 percent of whom were naturalized or Canadian-born citizens—were stripped of their rights, categorized as "enemy aliens," and forcibly uprooted from their homes, many with only twenty-four hours' notice. In the chaos and terror of the moment, families were torn apart without the individual family members knowing where they would be incarcerated. Up and down the coast, the boats of Japanese Canadian fishermen were seized, and later the government took possession of the homes, businesses, and personal belongings of the uprooted Japanese Canadian community. Everything was sold without the consent of the owners, and the new restrictions on their individual freedoms and rights continued over the next seven years. When the catastrophe had subsided, the once thriving Japanese Canadian community on the west coast of British Columbia had been destroyed. The traces of that horrific event, euphemistically described by the government—even sometimes by Japanese Canadians themselves—as "the evacuation," have remained to this day. This mass uprooting bore no relation to our usual understanding of "evacuation" as a removal of persons threatened by dangers, and carried out for their own protection. The Japanese Canadians who were so forcibly torn from their communities and dispossessed had become strangers in their own native land, Canada.

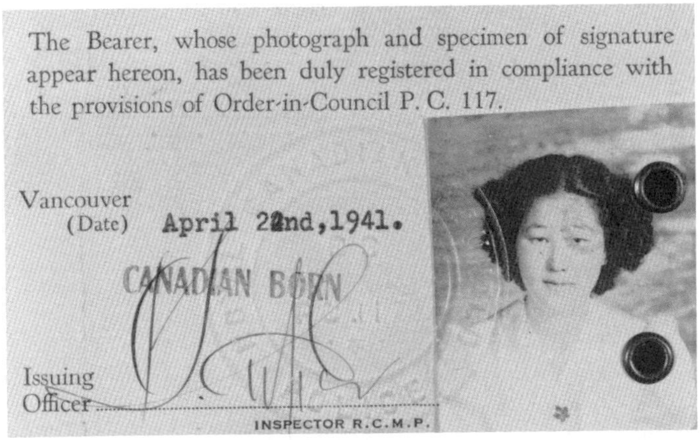

The Bearer, whose photograph and specimen of signature appear hereon, has been duly registered in compliance with the provisions of Order-in-Council P. C. 117.

Vancouver
(Date) April 22nd, 1941.

CANADIAN BORN

Issuing
Officer _____
INSPECTOR R.C.M.P.

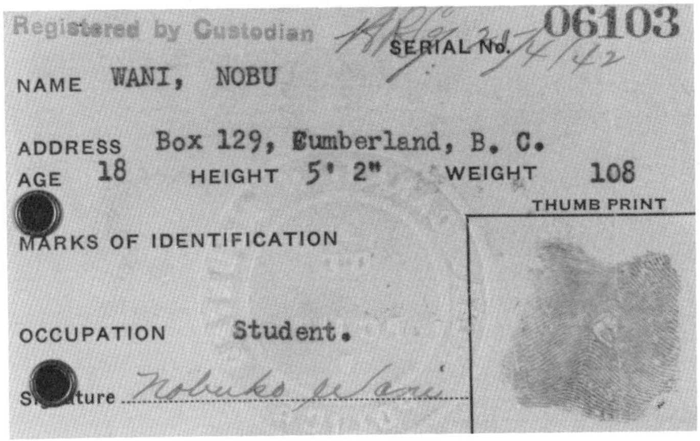

Registered by Custodian   SERIAL No. 06103

NAME   WANI, NOBU

ADDRESS   Box 129, Cumberland, B. C.

AGE 18   HEIGHT 5' 2"   WEIGHT   108

THUMB PRINT

MARKS OF IDENTIFICATION

OCCUPATION   Student.

Signature Nobuko Wani

This card belonging to nisei Nobu (Wani) Matsui was printed in The Case for Redress: Information *(NAJC, 1984), a press kit accompanying the NAJC's brief* Democracy Betrayed.
Courtesy of Nobu Matsui.

Japanese Canadians reading the removal notice posted outside the New Canadian *newspaper office on Powell Street, Vancouver.*
Photo: Vancouver Public Library #1343.

"*Okay we move. But where? Signs up on all highways...JAPS KEEP OUT. Curfew. 'My father is dying. May I have permission to go to his bedside? NO!' Like moles we burrow within after dark, and only dare to peek out of the window or else be thrown into the hoosegow with long term sentences and hard labour.*"

Muriel Kitagawa, from a letter to her brother Wes Fujiwara, March 4, 1942, This Is My Own *(Talonbooks, 1985).*

The uprooting of Japanese Canadians in 1942 was not an isolated act of racism, but the culmination of discriminatory attitudes directed towards them from the early days of settlement. The war itself offered the opportune moment for many powerful politicians, business and labour groups, and individuals in BC, to attack the social and economic base of the thriving Japanese Canadian community, under the guise of national security. Indeed, for many decades before, Japanese Canadians, as well as Chinese and Indo-Canadians, had been constantly harassed by many racists in BC. Older Japanese Canadians remembered well

17

Windows broken at K. Okada's store during the anti-Asian riot in the Powell Street district of the Japanese Canadian community, Vancouver, September 1907. *Photo: Japanese Canadian Cultural Centre, Toronto.*

Japanese Canadian being registered at Hastings Park, from the Vancouver Daily Province. *Photo: Vancouver Public Library #1344.*

the Vancouver riot of September 7, 1907, when a crowd at an anti-Asian rally suddenly turned into a mob, stormed through Chinatown breaking store windows, and were finally beaten back at Powell Street by a group of Japanese Canadians.

Before the uprooting, over 95 percent of Japanese Canadians lived in BC. During the sixty-five years since the first settler from Japan, Manzo Nagano, came to Canada in 1877, legal restrictions in BC not only disenfranchised Japanese Canadians, but also prevented them from holding public office and from entering mainstream professions such as law, pharmacy, teaching and accounting. Excluded from Canadian society at large, yet determined to create a place for themselves in this country, they established themselves in resource industries. By the 1930s, the issei, the first generation of Japanese Canadians, had built communities around the fishing and lumber industries, in the town of Steveston at the mouth of the Fraser River, and in towns and settlements along the coast and on Vancouver Island. Lucrative berry farms and market gardens had been developed in many areas of the Fraser Valley. In Vancouver, in the district around Powell Street, called "Nihonjin-machi" ("Japanese Town"), they lived, worked and shopped in a bustling urban centre of shops, hotels, restaurants and residential homes.

As the second-generation nisei came of age in the late 1930s, they appeared to be on the verge of reaping the economic benefits of their issei parents' labours. While still denied the vote in BC, as the Canadian-born children of immigrant parents, the nisei were educated to believe in democratic principles and civil liberties, and so were hopeful that the racist barriers which had always been imposed on them would eventually be lifted. At the outset of the next decade, however, their optimism was severely undermined—and their faith in Canadian democracy was tested to its very limits. Shortly after the bombing of Pearl Harbor on December 7, 1941, the entire social and economic fabric of this Japanese Canadian community was dismantled by the actions of their government.

The Terms "Issei," "Nisei," and "Sansei"

Japanese Canadians have named each generation in Canada, the immigrants from Japan being the "first generation." This differs from other ethnic groups for whom the first Canadian-born generation is the "first generation."

ISSEI

are the pioneers from Japan who chose Canada as their home. Japanese males immigrated from about 1877 to 1907, and most women came after 1908. Those who came after World War II are called "new immigrants," or "shinijusha."

NISEI

or second generation, are the Canadian-born children of the issei.

SANSEI

or third generation, are the children of the nisei, largely born in the 1940s and 50s.

YONSEI and GOSEI

are the fourth and fifth generations respectively. Most sansei have not married Japanese Canadians, perhaps due to pressure to assimilate after the uprooting, so their children are less visibly of Japanese ancestry.

RCMP officer posting the removal notice "To Male Enemy Aliens."
Photo: Vancouver Public Library #1342.

THE MASS UPROOTING

Just days after the bombing, Japanese-language newspapers were closed down and fishing boats were impounded, putting some 1,800 Japanese Canadian fishermen out of work. These first restrictions were seen by members of the community as needless and

Fishing boats impounded by the Royal Canadian Navy at Annieville Dyke on the Fraser River, 1941. In all, about 1,200 boats were seized and sold by order in council during January-February 1942. Photo: Vancouver Public Library #3190.

unfounded "precautionary measures" taken by a government caught up in the war hysteria of the time; nevertheless, they believed that no further measures would be taken if they tolerated this over-reaction and reminded the Canadian government that they were, after all, Canadian citizens. They were certainly not prepared for the Liberal government's decisions following swiftly on these first two restrictions.

As citizens loyal to this country, Japanese

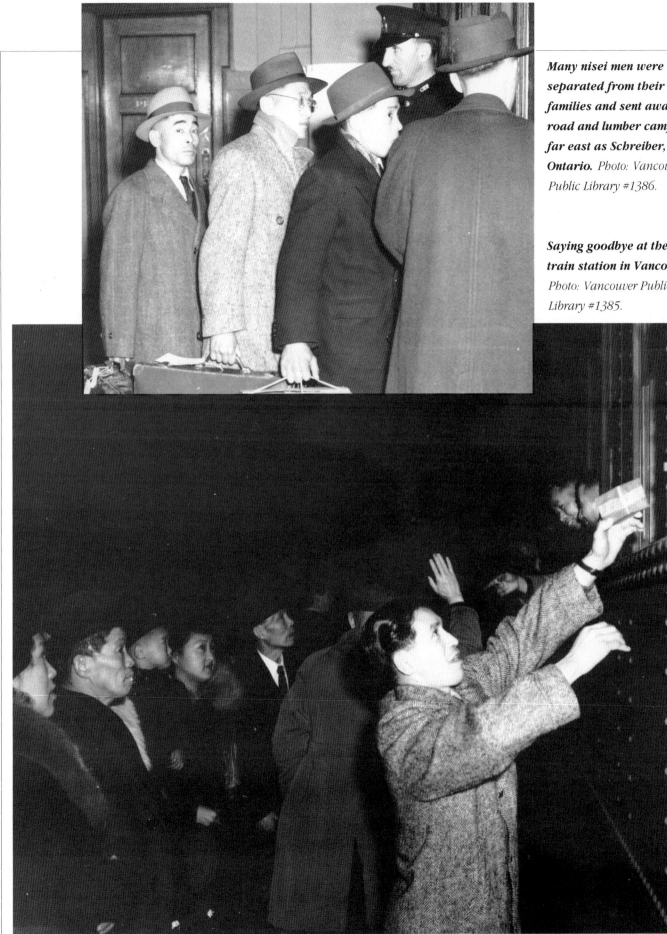

Many nisei men were separated from their families and sent away to road and lumber camps, as far east as Schreiber, Ontario. Photo: Vancouver Public Library #1386.

Saying goodbye at the CNR train station in Vancouver. Photo: Vancouver Public Library #1385.

Japanese Canadians arriving by train in Slocan City. *Photo: National Archives of Canada C137793.*

Canadians had assumed that their government would recognize their civil liberties. An editorial of January 4, 1942, in the community's newspaper, the *New Canadian*, dismissed as "silly" the rumours that they might be expelled from BC. Editor Tom Shoyama added, "The idea of camps equivalent to internment camps is also branded in the same light."

The first premonition of disaster came on January 14, when the government passed Order in Council PC 365 which designated an area 100-miles inland from the west coast as a "protected area." All male Japanese nationals aged 18 to 45 were to be removed from this zone and taken to road camps in the Jasper area of BC. Even this order, though considered extreme and unnecessary, was tolerated by most nisei—as "aliens," Japanese male nationals could be expected to accept some restrictions. Moreover, assurances had been given by the government that PC 365 was only a temporary "security measure," and that Canadians of Japanese ancestry need not fear such treatment.

TO MALE ENEMY ALIENS
NOTICE

Under date of February 2nd, 1942, the Honourable the Minister of National Defence with the concurrence of the Minister of Justice gave public notice defining an area of British Columbia, as described below, to be a protected area after the 31st day of January, 1942; that is to say, that area of the Province of British Columbia, including all islands, west of a line described hereunder:-

Commencing at boundary point No. 7 on the International Boundary between the Dominion of Canada and Alaska, thence following the line of the "Cascade Mountains" as defined by paragraph 2 of Section 24 of the Interpretation Act of British Columbia, being Chapter 1 of the Revised Statutes of 1936, to the Northwest corner of Lot 13-10, Range 5, Coast Land Districts, thence due East to a point due North of the Northwest corner of Lot 373, Range 5, Coast Land District, thence due South to said Northwest corner of Lot 373 being a point on the aforementioned line of the "Cascade Mountains", (being the area surrounding the village municipality of Terrace); thence following said line of the "Cascade Mountains" to the Western Boundary of Township 5, Range 26, West of the 6th Meridian, thence following the Northerly, Easterly and Southerly Boundaries of said Township 5, to the Southwest corner thereof, being a point on the line of the "Cascade Mountains" (being the area surrounding the village municipality of Hope); thence following the "Cascade Mountains" to the Southerly boundary of the Province.

Pursuant to the provisions of Regulation 4 of the Defence of Canada Regulations, the Minister of Justice has, on the 5th day of February, 1942, ordered that:-

1. All male Enemy Aliens of the ages of 18 years to 45 years, inclusive, shall leave the protected area hereinbefore referred to on or before the 1st day of April, 1942;

2. That, subject to the provisions of paragraph No. 1 of this Order, no Enemy Alien shall, after the date of this order, enter, leave or return to such protected area except with the permission of the Commissioner of the Royal Canadian Mounted Police Force, or an Officer of that Force designated by the Commissioner to act for him in this respect;

3. That no Enemy Alien shall have in his possession or use, while in such protected area, any camera, radio transmitter, radio short-wave receiving set, firearm, ammunition, or explosive.

S.T. WOOD (Commissioner)
Royal Canadian Mounted Police

OTTAWA, February 7, 1942.
TO BE POSTED IN A CONSPICUOUS PLACE

Order in Council PC 365, passed on January 16, 1942, ordered the removal of male Japanese Nationals living within the designated 100-mile "protected area" along the BC coast.

NOTICE

TO ALL PERSONS OF JAPANESE RACIAL ORIGIN

Having reference to the Protected Area of British Columbia as described in an Extra of the Canada Gazette, No. 174 dated Ottawa, Monday, February 2, 1942:-

1. EVERY PERSON OF THE JAPANESE RACE, WHILE WITHIN THE PROTECTED AREA AFORESAID, SHALL HEREAFTER BE AT HIS USUAL PLACE OF RESIDENCE EACH DAY BEFORE SUNSET AND SHALL REMAIN THEREIN UNTIL SUNRISE ON THE FOLLOWING DAY, AND NO SUCH PERSON SHALL GO OUT OF HIS USUAL PLACE OF RESIDENCE AFORESAID UPON THE STREETS OR OTHERWISE DURING THE HOURS BETWEEN SUNSET AND SUNRISE;

2. NO PERSON OF THE JAPANESE RACE SHALL HAVE IN HIS POSSESSION OR USE IN SUCH PROTECTED AREA ANY MOTOR VEHICLE, CAMERA, RADIO TRANSMITTER, RADIO RECEIVING SET, FIREARM, AMMUNITION OR EXPLOSIVE;

3. IT SHALL BE THE DUTY OF EVERY PERSON OF THE JAPANESE RACE HAVING IN HIS POSSESSION OR UPON HIS PREMISES ANY ARTICLE MENTIONED IN THE NEXT PRECEDING PARAGRAPH, FORTHWITH TO CAUSE SUCH ARTICLE TO BE DELIVERED UP TO ANY JUSTICE OF THE PEACE RESIDING IN OR NEAR THE LOCALITY WHERE ANY SUCH ARTICLE IS HAD IN POSSESSION, OR TO AN OFFICER OR CONSTABLE OF THE POLICE FORCE OF THE PROVINCE OR CITY IN OR NEAR SUCH LOCALITY OR TO AN OFFICER OR CONSTABLE OF THE ROYAL CANADIAN MOUNTED POLICE.

4. ANY JUSTICE OF THE PEACE OR OFFICER OR CONSTABLE RECEIVING ANY ARTICLE MENTIONED IN PARAGRAPH 2 OF THIS ORDER SHALL GIVE TO THE PERSON DELIVERING THE SAME A RECEIPT THEREFOR AND SHALL REPORT THE FACT TO THE COMMISSIONER OF THE ROYAL CANADIAN MOUNTED POLICE, AND SHALL RETAIN OR OTHERWISE DISPOSE OF ANY SUCH ARTICLE AS DIRECTED BY THE SAID COMMISSIONER.

5. ANY PEACE OFFICER OR ANY OFFICER OR CONSTABLE OF THE ROYAL CANADIAN MOUNTED POLICE HAVING POWER TO ACT AS SUCH PEACE OFFICER OR OFFICER OR CONSTABLE IN THE SAID PROTECTED AREA, IS AUTHORIZED TO SEARCH WITHOUT WARRANT THE PREMISES OR ANY PLACE OCCUPIED OR BELIEVED TO BE OCCUPIED BY ANY PERSON OF THE JAPANESE RACE REASONABLY SUSPECTED OF HAVING IN HIS POSSESSION OR UPON HIS PREMISES ANY ARTICLE MENTIONED IN PARAGRAPH 2 OF THIS ORDER, AND TO SEIZE ANY SUCH ARTICLE FOUND ON SUCH PREMISES;

6. EVERY PERSON OF THE JAPANESE RACE SHALL LEAVE THE PROTECTED AREA AFORESAID FORTHWITH;

7. NO PERSON OF THE JAPANESE RACE SHALL ENTER SUCH PROTECTED AREA EXCEPT UNDER PERMIT ISSUED BY THE ROYAL CANADIAN MOUNTED POLICE;

8. IN THIS ORDER, "PERSONS OF THE JAPANESE RACE" MEANS, AS WELL AS ANY PERSON WHOLLY OF THE JAPANESE RACE, A PERSON NOT WHOLLY OF THE JAPANESE RACE IF HIS FATHER OR MOTHER IS OF THE JAPANESE RACE AND IF THE COMMISSIONER OF THE ROYAL CANADIAN MOUNTED POLICE BY NOTICE IN WRITING HAS REQUIRED OR REQUIRES HIM TO REGISTER PURSUANT TO ORDER-IN-COUNCIL P.C. 9760 OF DECEMBER 16th, 1941.

DATED AT OTTAWA THIS 26th DAY OF FEBRUARY, 1942.

Louis S. St. Laurent,
Minister of Justice

To be posted in a Conspicuous Place

Order in Council PC 1486, passed on February 24, 1942, authorized the removal of all "persons of Japanese racial origin" and gave the RCMP the power to search without warrant, enforce a dusk-to-dawn curfew, and to confiscate cars, radios, cameras, and firearms.

> *"From the army point of view, I cannot see that Japanese Canadians constitute the slightest menace to national security."*
>
> Major General Ken Stuart, quoted in Democracy Betrayed (NAJC, 1984).

> *"Take them back to Japan. They do not belong here, and there is only one solution to the problem. They cannot be assimilated as Canadians for no matter how long the Japanese remàin in Canada they will always be Japanese."*
>
> Thomas Reid, Liberal Member of Parliament for New Westminster, in a speech to the East Burnaby Liberal Association, January 15, 1942, quoted in Democracy Betrayed (NAJC, 1984).

The Term "Internment"

As Ann Sunahara points out, "Legally ...the nisei could not be interned. They were Canadian citizens and internment under the Geneva Convention is a legal act applicable only to aliens..." (Politics of Racism, p. 66). Aware of this, the Canadian government carefully chose their words, saying that Japanese Canadians were being "detained at the pleasure of the Minister of Justice," Louis St. Laurent. Had they been "interned," their rights would have been protected by international law. Instead, the "detained" Japanese Canadians were stripped of their rights with no means of appeal—and they were also required to pay for their own "internment." To this day, they continue to view their uprooting and dispossession as internment.

Within three weeks—with a shock that threw the Japanese Canadian community into tumult—Order in Council PC 1486 was passed, expanding the power of the Minister of Justice to remove any and all persons from a designated protected zone. This blanket power was then applied to one group alone—"all persons of Japanese racial origin." This new policy radically altered the status of Japanese Canadians. From February 25, 1942, their Canadian birthright became meaningless, and henceforth they were to be judged solely on the basis of their racial ancestry, not on their citizenship, or even the country of their birth. The War Measures Act legalized the government actions, even though they were based on racist precepts and not necessary by military standards for national security. The stigma of "enemy alien" made Japanese Canadians outcasts in their own country.

On March 4, 1942, the BC Security Commission was established, chaired by Vancouver industrialist Austin Taylor, with RCMP Assistant Commissioner Frederick J. Mead and Assistant Commissioner of the BC Provincial Police, John Shirras. It was this civilian body that was empowered to carry out the systematic expulsion of "all persons of Japanese racial origin" from the area within 100 miles of the BC coast. A "Custodian of Enemy Property" was authorized to administer and hold "in trust" the properties and belongings of these people.

As the uprooting began, a dusk-to-dawn curfew was imposed on all Japanese Canadians. Houses could be entered at all times of the day and night and searched by RCMP officers without a warrant. Cameras and radios were confiscated, cars impounded, and removal notices were handed out.

Thousands of Japanese Canadians, rounded up like cattle, were herded into Vancouver from the coastal towns and Vancouver Island. Many had

24

The War Measures Act in the 1940s

During World War II, the government invoked the War Measures Act which transferred the powers of Parliament to the Governor in Council or, effectively, to the cabinet. The actions against Japanese Canadians, including expulsion from the 100-mile "protected area," internment, seizure and sale of property, and exile to Japan, were all done through orders in council passed by cabinet. Although cabinet reported to Parliament as a courtesy from time to time, Parliament had little idea of what was being done to Japanese Canadians. For example, cabinet advised that Japanese Canadian property was being held in trust, and was being sold if necessary to prevent losses from deterioration. Cabinet did not reveal the plan to sell all land and personal property of Japanese Canadians within the 100-mile zone. By the time it became publicly known, several months later, that all property was to be sold, it was too late.

The War Measures Act provided an opportunity for abuse of power. Although Parliament can rarely stop the actions of a majority government, the public accountability of the parliamentary process helps prevent the abuse of legislative powers. For example, the Mackenzie King government knew that there would be opposition to exiling Japanese Canadians to Japan after the war was over. At first, the power to deport was slipped into the National Emergency Transitional Powers Act of 1945, known as Bill 15, an Act used to facilitate the removal of wartime economic restrictions under the War Measures Act. When Parliament vocally opposed the inclusion of such a ministerial power, that clause was withdrawn from the Bill. However, to circumvent further opposition, cabinet passed an order in council just before the expiry of the War Measures Act. Orders in council made under the War Measures Act were extended automatically and could not be touched by Parliament. Thus Mackenzie King's government gave themselves the power to deport Japanese Canadians after the war—even though they knew Parliament did not approve.

Confiscated cars at Hastings Park were later sold off at bargain prices by the Custodian of Enemy Property. Photo: Vancouver Public Library #1369.

Children's dining room at Hastings Park. *Photo: Vancouver Public Library #14925.*

"Father and mother were taken to a so-called sick bay, a partitioned six by eight foot horse stall with twin beds for each couple. The stench from years of horse urine soaked in the floors was enough to make a healthy person ill."

Tom Tagami, from Justice in Our Time *(NAJC, 1988).*

In an attempt to create privacy, women and children hung blankets and sheets around their bunks at Hastings Park.
Photo: Vancouver Public Library #14923.

Communal women's washroom at Hastings Park. *Photo: Vancouver Public Library #14927.*

been given as little as twenty-four hours to vacate their homes. Chaos, terror and disbelief infected the community as families were split apart and men were hastily shipped off to road camps. In Vancouver, Hastings Park with its Pacific National Exhibition (PNE) buildings, was used as a "clearing site" before people were shipped away from the coast. Conditions in the park were degrading and barbaric; the women and children were segregated and some forced to live in the

Livestock Buildings. Many of these unfortunate individuals were confined there for months, eating substandard food, without knowing where they would end up or what had become of their husbands, families, and relatives.

Meanwhile, some areas and towns in the BC interior were quickly prepared as internment centres: Greenwood, Sandon, Kaslo, New Denver, Rosebery, Slocan City, Bay Farm, Popoff, and Lemon Creek. One site, Tashme, was constructed on vacant land just outside of the 100-mile "protected area," close to Hope, its name an acronym for the three members of the BC Security Commission: TAylor, SHirras, MEad.

Matt Matsui taking stock of his bikes in his Vancouver shop at the time of the uprooting. He now owns Grove Cycle in Toronto and was active in the redress movement. Photo: Vancouver Public Library #1365.

One of many letters sent by the RCMP to individuals, giving them less than twenty-four hours' notice to leave the coast.

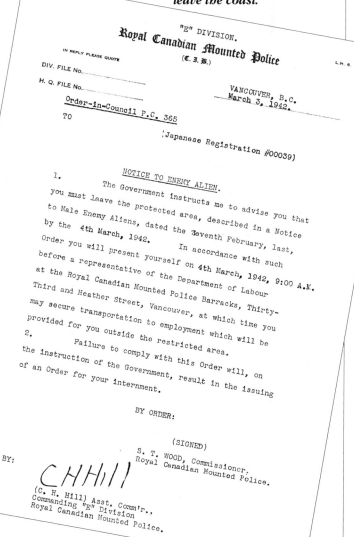

"E" DIVISION.
Royal Canadian Mounted Police
(C. I. B.)

L.H. 6.

IN REPLY PLEASE QUOTE

DIV. FILE No.............

H. Q. FILE No.............

VANCOUVER, B.C.
March 3, 1942.

Order-in-Council P.C. 365

TO

(Japanese Registration #00039)

NOTICE TO ENEMY ALIEN.

1. The Government instructs me to advise you that you must leave the protected area, described in a Notice to Male Enemy Aliens, dated the Seventh February, last, by the 4th March, 1942. In accordance with such Order you will present yourself on 4th March, 1942, 9:00 A.M. before a representative of the Department of Labour at the Royal Canadian Mounted Police Barracks, Thirty-Third and Heather Street, Vancouver, at which time you may secure transportation to employment which will be provided for you outside the restricted area.

2. Failure to comply with this Order will, on the instruction of the Government, result in the issuing of an Order for your internment.

BY ORDER:

(SIGNED)
S. T. WOOD, Commissioner,
Royal Canadian Mounted Police.

BY:

CHHill

(C. H. Hill) Asst. Commr.,
Commanding "E" Division
Royal Canadian Mounted Police.

The New Canadian

THE VOICE OF THE SECOND GENERATION

Vol. V, No. 24 [A]   VANCOUVER, B. C.   THURS., FEB. 26, 1942

Ottawa Orders Dusk To Dawn Cur

ot Yet Confirmed Here

rder to Remain in Homes
To Be Worked Out Soon

VANCOUVER, Feb. 26.—The Canadian Press this ....noon carried an Ottawa dispatch saying that all Japan- ....living within the British Columbia Protected Area must ......ain in their homes between sunset and sunrise, under ....order approved by the Dominion Government today.

While additional details remain to be worked out, ...als of the Department of Justice said, the order is ....ected to go into effect almost immediately.

The order applies only to all persons of the Japanese ......living in the protected area, first and second genera- ...., along the British Columbia coast and the islands. They ...t return to their usual places of residence before dark, ...rding to the order.

It would not go into effect until official notice of it is ...ted, however.   R.C.M.P. officials said today they had ......eived no inormation on the new order.

The curfew, it is said, is designed to restrict move- ....ts of all persons of Japanese origin until they are moved ....nd.

MOVE ALL JAPANESE
ULTIMATE GOVT. PLAN

OTTAWA.—Naturalized and Canadian-born Japan- ....will be removed from the British Columbia protected .....a as well as Japanese nationals, Labor Minister Hum- ....ey Mitchell told a press conference Wednesday night.

Ultimately, the minister said, the government intended ....move every person of Japanese origin, male and female, ...d of all ages from the protected area.

Workers In Construction Corps
To Receive Dollar Per Day

OTTAWA.—Formation of a Japanese Canadian con- ....uction corps for employment in war-time projects "with- ....or without" Canada was announced Wednesday by ....me Minister King.

Basic pay of the corps will be $1 per day with depen- ....t allowances at the rate of 50 per cent allowed to armed ....ces with a bonus at the end of the war of $2 for every ....nth served. Enlistment in the corps is for the duration.

The New Canadia

396 Powell Street   Vancouver, B. C.   PA

A paper published by and for second generation Japanese and devoted to their welfare as citizens of Canad

40c month; 6 mos: $2.25 in advance; One year: $4.00
Published tri-weekly at the Taiyo Printing Comp

*Front page of the Japanese
Canadian community
newspaper, the New
Canadian, announcing the
mass uprooting,
February 24, 1942.*

(top) **During the first winter
in the internment camp at
Slocan, many Japanese
Canadians had to live in
tents.** *Photo: Vancouver
Japanese Canadian Citizens'
Association, Redress Committee.*

(above) **Internment houses
covered with tar paper at
Tashme.** *Photo: University of
British Columbia, Special
Collections.*

Kyoshi Kay Shimizu

Nisei Kyoshi (Kato) Shimizu, as a young graduate student in the School of Social Work at UBC, assisted at Hastings Park and later helped set up a welfare office in Kaslo. She moved to Toronto in 1943, and a year later married Kunio Shimizu, well known as secretary and interpreter for the Japanese Canadian Citizens' Council (JCCC), and one of three nisei representatives on the committee of community advisors to the BC Security Commission.

After Kunio's death in 1982, Kyoshi became involved in the redress movement and chaired the Ottawa Redress Committee in 1985. She then moved to Vancouver where she joined the Vancouver JCCA Redress Committee, and in 1988 settled in Victoria.

In a speech at the Vancouver Redress Rally, in March 1988, she recalled her efforts as a social worker in Vancouver:

"I will never forget the scene in the Livestock Building where the women and children were being housed. There was that indescribable smell of manure and disinfectant, the cries and whimpers of children desperately hanging on to their mothers' skirts, the bewildered looks on many faces, the pathetic attempts to create some privacy between the rows of army cots. I was in a state of shock, unable to think or act. Finally, one of the older women—a Japanese school teacher—suggested that I take a group of children outside, and helped round up a few for a game of ring-around-the-rosy, so their mothers could get on with their unpacking."

Kyoshi and Kunio Shimizu in Toronto, 1946, two years after they were married.
Both photos courtesy of Kyoshi Shimizu.

29

Japanese Canadians in Internment Camps in British Columbia

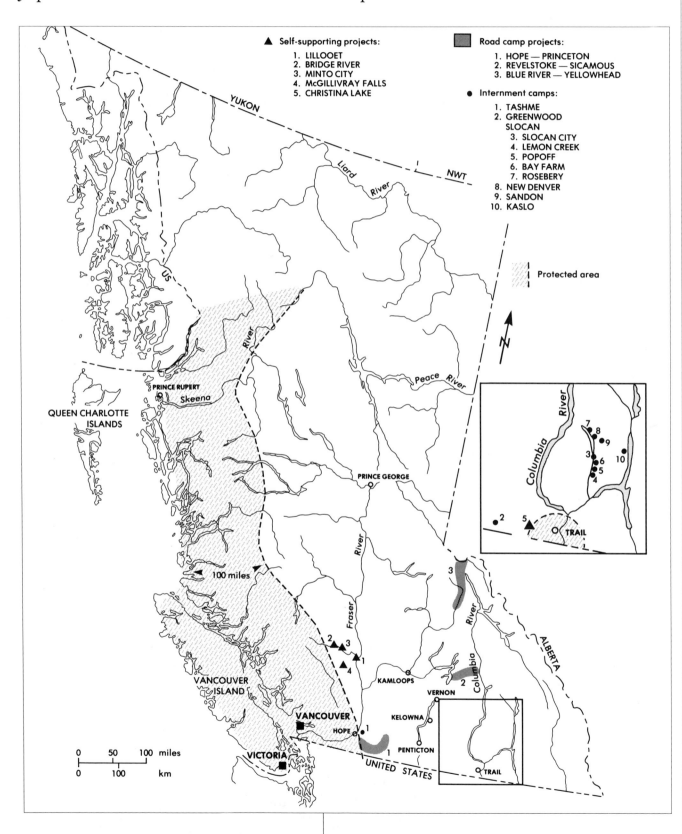

▲ Self-supporting projects:
1. LILLOOET
2. BRIDGE RIVER
3. MINTO CITY
4. McGILLIVRAY FALLS
5. CHRISTINA LAKE

▨ Road camp projects:
1. HOPE — PRINCETON
2. REVELSTOKE — SICAMOUS
3. BLUE RIVER — YELLOWHEAD

● Internment camps:
1. TASHME
2. GREENWOOD
    SLOCAN
    3. SLOCAN CITY
    4. LEMON CREEK
    5. POPOFF
    6. BAY FARM
    7. ROSEBERY
8. NEW DENVER
9. SANDON
10. KASLO

Protected area

Distribution of Japanese Canadian Population After the Mass Uprooting from the 100-mile Coastal Zone (as of October 31, 1942)

Road construction camps:	945*
Blue River - Yellowhead	258
Revelstoke - Sicamous	346
Hope - Princeton	296
Schreiber	32
Black Spur	13

Sugar beet farms:	3,991
Alberta	2,588
Manitoba	1,053
Ontario (males only)	350

Camps in BC	12,029
Greenwood	1,177
Slocan Valley	4,814
Sandon	933
Kaslo	964
Tashme	2,636
New Denver	1,505

Self-supporting sites	1,161
Special permits to approved employment	1,359
Repatriated to Japan	42
Uprooted prior to March 1942	579
Interned in prisoner of war camps in Ontario	699
In detention in Vancouver	111
Hastings Park hospital	105

TOTAL	**21,460****

*Between March and June 1942, a total of 2,161 Japanese Canadians were placed in road construction camps. Many of them subsequently were allowed to join families in the interior detention camps by October 1942.

**92 persons, representing Japanese Canadians married to non-Japanese Canadians and their children, were issued permits April 11, 1942, exempting them from uprooting orders.

Sources: Canada, BC Security Commission, *Removal of Japanese from Protected Areas* (October 31, 1942); Ken Adachi, *The Enemy That Never Was*.

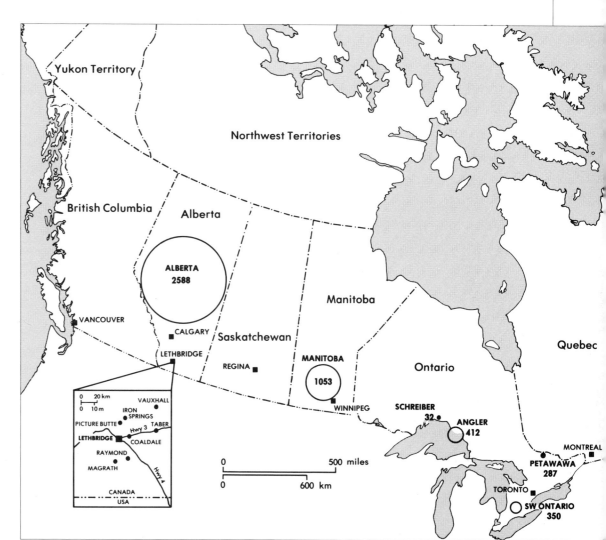

Aerial view of camp at Lemon Creek. Photo: *Vancouver Japanese Canadian Citizens' Association, Redress Committee.*

31

Japanese Canadian Population Distribution by Provinces in 1941 and 1947

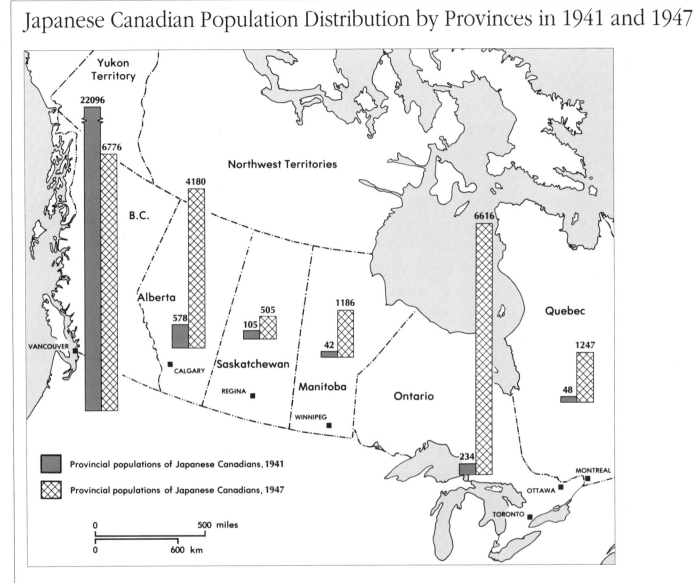

Distribution of Japanese Canadians by Province, 1941-1951

Province	1941	1942	1943	1944	1945	1946	1947	1951
BC	22,096	21,975	16,504	16,103	15,610	14,716	6,776	7,169
Alberta	578	534	3,231	3,469	3,559	3,681	4,180	3,336
Saskatchewan	105	100	129	153	157	164	505	225
Manitoba	42	30	1,084	1,094	1,052	1,052	1,186	1,161
Ontario	234	132	1,650	2,424	2,914	3,742	6,616	8,581
Quebec	48	25	96	344	532	716	1,247	1,137
New Brunswick	3	—	—	—	—	10	10	7
PEI	—	—	—	—	—	—	6	6
Nova Scotia	2	2	1	1	1	1	1	4
Newfoundland	—	—	—	—	—	—	—	2
Yukon & NWT	41	39	30	29	29	30	31	35
TOTAL	**23,149**	**22,837**	**22,725**	**23,617**	**23,854**	**24,112**	**20,558**	**21,663**

Source: Audrey Kobayashi, *A Demographic Profile of Japanese Canadians*, (Department of the Secretary of State, 1989), p. 6.

Kome Nagasaki

Kome is a shy, soft-spoken nisei woman who was born in Vancouver in 1903. She has never visited Japan and has no desire to do so.

"At the age of 18, Kome married. After years of hard labour, she and her husband poured their life's savings into the purchase of a three-bedroom house at 1941 Turner Street in Vancouver. They moved into their new home on December 6, 1941. On the morning of December 8 they responded with shock and outrage to the radio announcement that Japan had bombed Pearl Harbor.

"In January 1942, Kome's husband was fired from his job at a lumber mill in Marpole and Kome lost her job when the Japanese Canadian-owned clothing factory where she worked was shut down. At the end of March, her husband was sent away to forced labour at a road camp in Jasper. On April 21, 1942, Kome, her sister and her aging mother were sent to Greenwood, a detention centre in the Interior of British Columbia. Kome's 21-year-old son, John, was an idealistic sansei (third generation) youth with a strong faith in democracy. Concerned about his mother's safety, he refused to leave British Columbia. Ten days after Kome left, he was arrested on Powell Street in Vancouver, charged with delaying his departure, and placed behind barbed wire in a prisoner of war camp in Petawawa, Ontario."

The profile of "Kome" was one of three profiles published in the NAJC's redress brief Democracy Betrayed *(NAJC, 1984) to show the personal impact of the mass uprooting. Kome's new house and possessions were sold without her consent. Her experience reflected the lives of many, especially women, whose families were torn apart by order of the BC Security Commission. Today Kome Nagasaki lives in Toronto. Both her husband and her son died years before the Redress Settlement.*
Photo: Waylen Miki.

Inside an internment house heated with a stove made from an oil drum.
Photo: Japanese Canadian Cultural Centre, Toronto.

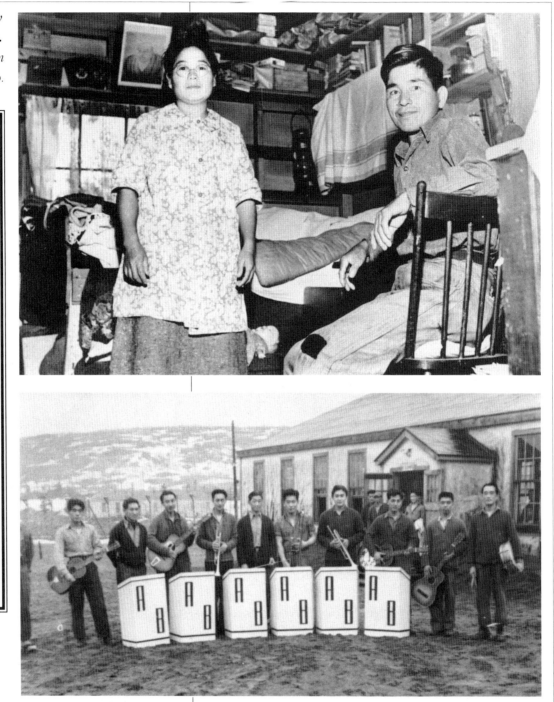

Couple in their tiny bedroom at Lemon Creek.
Photo: Japanese Canadian Cultural Centre, Toronto.

Band in prisoner of war camp at Angler, Ontario.
Photo: Roy Kawamoto Collection.

"*There were crowds of people, farmers and newsmen. We tried to hide to avoid having our pictures taken. Wagons, horses, and tractors waited to take us. It was like some slave trading market. We were terrified, not knowing where we were going. Some didn't want to move. Women were crying. The farmers hurried us...*"

Mr. & Mrs. Eiji Tashiro, from A Dream of Riches (*Japanese Canadian Centennial Project, 1978*), p. 112.

Initially, the BC Security Commission appointed Etsuji Morii, a naturalized issei, to form a "Japanese Liaison Committee," in the hopes of securing, quickly and efficiently, the co-operation of the community. They could not have made a worse choice. For many years before, Morii had been mistrusted, intensely disliked, and even feared by Japanese Canadians. He had a notorious

Road camp at Three Forks River. *Courtesy of Tak Nishino.*

> "*You should have seen the house we used to live in. Just one layer of siding, that's all, and a wood stove to heat the house. It was about 20 by 12 feet, every room just a hanging curtain. In the winter our bed froze solid and the blankets all stuck to the side...The first year we came it went down to almost 43 below. We just burned wood all night long. The house wasn't insulated. I don't know how we stood it, really, when we look back.*"
>
> Mrs. Hirayama, on winter in Manitoba, from A Dream of Riches (*Japanese Canadian Centennial Project, 1978*), p. 115.

reputation as the owner of a gambling house, and it was rumoured that he belonged to the Black Dragon Society, a Japanese nationalist underworld organization. Outraged that such an individual had been chosen to represent them, some Japanese Canadians reacted by forming two groups: the Naturalized Canadian Japanese Association (NCJA), for the issei, and the Japanese Canadian Citizens Council (JCCC), for the nisei. Both groups advocated co-operation with the BC Security Commission, but rejected Morii as their representative. As a result of their protests to the BC Security Commission, three nisei from the JCCC were added to the Japanese Liaison Committee, Tom Shoyama, Kunio Shimizu, and Chitose Uchida. However, while Morii's power quickly waned, an even more volatile issue began to flare up.

Work crew clearing the forest for the Trans Canada Highway, at Three Forks River road camp, near **Revelstoke, BC.** *Courtesy of Tak Nishino.*

Many Japanese Canadians, especially younger nisei, looked upon the BC Security Commission's policy of breaking up families as unnecessary and cruel. At first, working within the JCCC, they requested removal in family units. When the BC Security Commission refused to change the policy, they became more aggressive and split away from the JCCC, forming another organization, the Nisei Mass Evacuation Group (NMEG). The JCCC continued to urge the community to co-operate with the Security Commission, but now their position was undermined by the NMEG who called for resistance to the government's removal order, at least until families

An advertisement for Japanese Canadian sugar beet workers. From Heather Robertson, Sugar Farmers of Manitoba *(Manitoba Beet Growers Association, 1968), p. 133.*

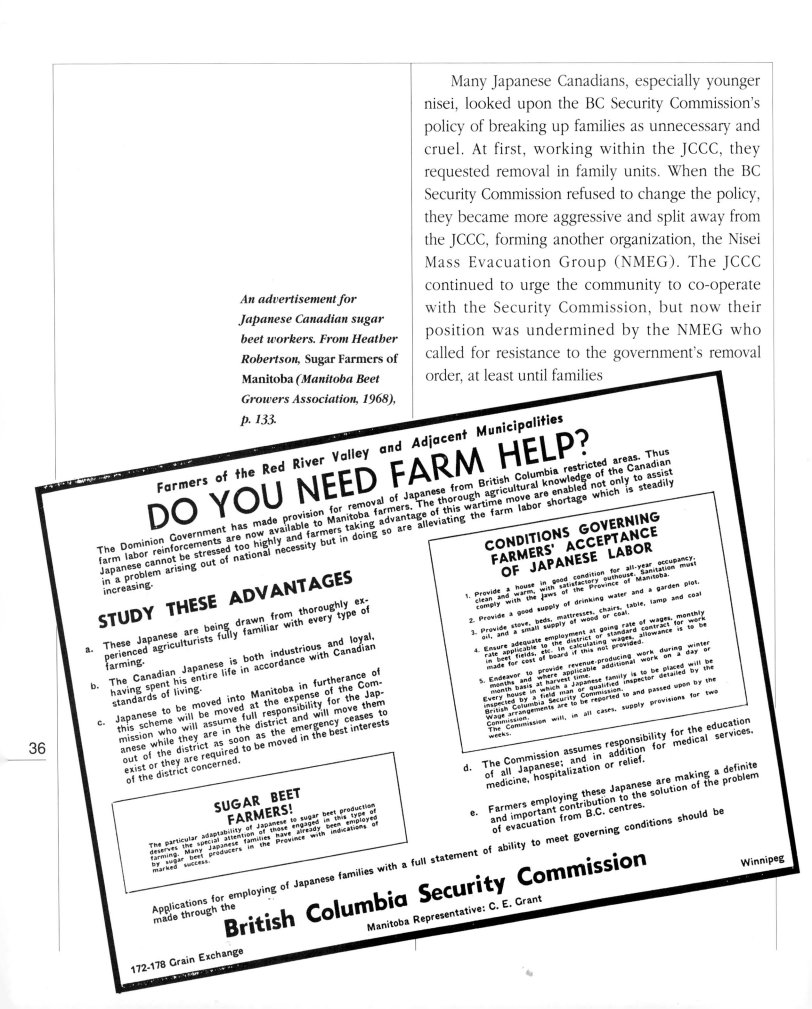

Farmers of the Red River Valley and Adjacent Municipalities

DO YOU NEED FARM HELP?

The Dominion Government has made provision for removal of Japanese from British Columbia restricted areas. Thus farm labor reinforcements are now available to Manitoba farmers. The thorough agricultural knowledge of the Canadian Japanese cannot be stressed too highly and farmers taking advantage of this wartime move are enabled not only to assist in a problem arising out of national necessity but in doing so are alleviating the farm labor shortage which is steadily increasing.

STUDY THESE ADVANTAGES

a. These Japanese are being drawn from thoroughly experienced agriculturists fully familiar with every type of farming.

b. The Canadian Japanese is both industrious and loyal, having spent his entire life in accordance with Canadian standards of living.

c. Japanese to be moved into Manitoba in furtherance of this scheme will be moved at the expense of the Commission who will assume full responsibility for the Japanese while they are in the district and will move them out of the district as soon as the emergency ceases to exist or they are required to be moved in the best interests of the district concerned.

SUGAR BEET FARMERS!
The particular adaptability of Japanese to sugar beet production deserves the special attention of those engaged in this type of farming. Many Japanese families have already been employed by sugar beet producers in the Province with indications of marked success.

CONDITIONS GOVERNING FARMERS' ACCEPTANCE OF JAPANESE LABOR

1. Provide a house in good condition for all-year occupancy, clean and warm, with satisfactory outhouse. Sanitation must comply with the laws of the Province of Manitoba.

2. Provide a good supply of drinking water and a garden plot.

3. Provide stove, beds, mattresses, chairs, table, lamp and coal oil, and a small supply of wood or coal.

4. Ensure adequate employment at going rate of wages, monthly rate applicable to the district or standard contract for work in beet fields, etc. In calculating wages, allowance is to be made for cost of board if this not provided.

5. Endeavor to provide revenue-producing work during winter months and where applicable additional work on a day or month basis at harvest time.
   Every house in which a Japanese family is to be placed will be inspected by a field man or qualified inspector detailed by the British Columbia Security Commission.
   Wage arrangements are to be reported to and passed upon by the Commission.
   The Commission will, in all cases, supply provisions for two weeks.

d. The Commission assumes responsibility for the education of all Japanese; and in addition for medical services, medicine, hospitalization or relief.

e. Farmers employing these Japanese are making a definite and important contribution to the solution of the problem of evacuation from B.C. centres.

Applications for employing of Japanese families with a full statement of ability to meet governing conditions should be made through the

British Columbia Security Commission

Manitoba Representative: C. E. Grant

Winnipeg

172-178 Grain Exchange

Japanese Canadian girls in kimono for a Bon-Odori ("summer festival") at Greenwood, BC, during the internment. Photo: Japanese Canadian Cultural Centre, Toronto.

were allowed to remain together.

On March 25, 1942, when the first group of nisei men were given notices to go by train to Schreiber, Ontario, over 100 refused to go. They were rounded up by RCMP officers, confined in the Immigration Hall, and then sent to prisoner of war camps, first to Petawawa, then later to Angler, both in Ontario. Between April and June 1942, some 470 nisei were interned behind barbed wire in these camps, without being charged with any crime.

By July 1, 1942, the BC Security Commission finally instituted a policy of family re-unification.

By November 1942, some 22,000 Japanese Canadians had been forcibly uprooted from their west coast homes and communities. During the eight-month period beginning the previous March, the BC Security Commission had sought whatever means at their disposal to accomplish their mandate. A number of individuals with family connections in Japanese Canadian communities outside the protected area in BC, particularly in the Okanagan Valley, were allowed to move on their own. A few others with sponsors or relatives in eastern Canada were allowed to go east, also on

"...we have said 'YES' to all your previous orders, however unreasonable they might have seemed. But, we are firm in saying 'NO' to your last order which calls for break-up of our families.

"When we say 'NO' at this point, we request you to remember that we are British subjects by birth, that we are no less loyal to Canada than any other Canadian, that we have done nothing to deserve the break-up of our families, that we are law-abiding Canadian citizens, and that we are willing to accept suspension of our civil rights—rights to retain our homes and businesses, boats, cars, radios and cameras...In spite of that we have given up everything. In view of this sacrifice we feel that our request for mass evacuation in family groups will not seem unreasonable to you..."

From a letter to Austin Taylor, Chairman, BC Security Commission, from the Nisei Mass Evacuation Group; cited in This Is My Own (Talonbooks, 1985), p. 39.

"We were called the [Nisei] Mass Evacuation Group. We negotiated with the government and said we would go wherever they wanted only after we were sure our families were adjusted to their move. When the BC Security Commission refused our request, we refused to go. We were taken to the Immigration Shed, behind bars, and from there we were shipped in the dark of night to the internment camp where just before we arrived, 500 German prisoners of war had been kept. We were guarded 24 hours a day."

Michael Ochiai, from "40 Years of Waiting Over for Montreal Family," Barbara Newborn, The Senior Times (Montreal), October 1988.

their own recognizance. In total, some 1,350 were allowed to leave on "special permits" issued on an individual basis by the Security Commission.

In addition to these "sponsorship" arrangements, a small group, about 1,150, were given permission by the BC Security Commission to move to certain places in BC on what was termed a "self-supporting" basis. These were individuals with sufficient assets to assume full financial responsibility for their own move, their new housing, and living expenses, without requiring the aid of third party "sponsors." However, only a small minority of Japanese Canadians were offered the chance of becoming "self-supporting." The apparent choice and privilege implied by this "option" created enmity and bitterness within the remainder of the community. Japanese Canadians did not understand that the so-called "self-supporting" sites were the BC Security Commission's way of taking advantage of those who were willing and able to absorb all the costs of their own uprooting, even their moving and travelling expenses.

The vast majority of Japanese Canadians, however, were not able to choose where they wanted to go.

The BC Security Commission devised three major destinations for the dispersal of the remainder of Japanese Canadians from the coast. Early on, in March and April, some 1,000 men were placed at various road camps. The Japanese nationals went to camps around the BC/Alberta border, while the Canadian-born nisei ended up on the Hope/Princeton highway, or else were sent across Canada to Schreiber, Ontario. In the meantime, the Security Commission chose "ghost" towns in the BC interior, with empty buildings and adequate space for housing, to use as additional internment sites. Of the Japanese Canadian community that was uprooted, the largest group, some 12,000, were interned in camps in BC. Concurrently, a labour shortage on sugar beet farms in Alberta and Manitoba created a demand

> "*Connie Matsuo recalls standing with her husband in a Winnipeg hall 46 years ago while farmers chose laborers like cattle from a group of Japanese Canadians who had just arrived from British Columbia.*
> *'We were just about the last ones picked because we had two old parents and I had just had a baby.*'"

From "*Ottawa Apologizes to Internees,*" Winnipeg Free Press, *September 23, 1988.*

Japanese Canadians at Angler had to wear prison uniforms with circles on the back, used as a target when anyone tried to escape. Many of those interned were Canadian-born who had not complied with the BC Security Commission's order to leave the coast.
Photo: Roy Kawamoto Collection.

39

This postcard from Robert (Yukio) Shimoda, interned in a prisoner of war camp at Angler, Ontario, to his sister, bears the stamp of the censor and Prisoner of War frank. Shimoda was a leading figure in the Nisei Mass Evacuation Group.
Courtesy of Fumiko (Shimoda) Kanbara.

One of many newsletters distributed by the Nisei Mass Evacuation Group.
Courtesy of Tameo Kanbara.

April 27th, 1942

To Nisei:

We all have been bitterly aware of poor living conditions prevailing in the Hastings Park Manning Pool. This morning a concrete evidence of such conditions became undoubtedly apparent. The inmates could not stand the food any longer and went on hunger-strike as a protest.

The investigation disclosed amongst other things:

1. Insufficient quantity of food.
2. Improper quality of food.

It further disclosed:

1. The Security Commission and all the so-called Japanese laison committees are not fulfilling the responsibilities seriously enough.
2. They are not properly and systematically organized to carry out other responsibilities.
3. Private enterprises for food distributions are allowed. This only benefits a small minority of the inmates who can afford them.

The above mentioned state of affairs is only one example of what we are up against and seriously concerned with. This to-gether with other reasons is why we simply must insist on our demand for MASS EVACUATION IN FAMILY GROUPS.

We all have seen what those people who encouraged us to go to work camps leaving our families in their care, are doing and might do to our families when and if we go by ourselves.

Knowing this how can we leave our families? Knowing this how can we discontinue our demand for mass evacuation in family groups?

NISEI MASS EVACUATION GROUP

P. S.
We have been aware that gambling has always been allowed in the Manning Pool. Our investigation disclosed that as a result of such gambling, school children are imitating, and women and children are already suffering. Why do those people who claim to be responsible for the inmates' welfare continue to allow gambling.

REMEMBER:

1. Our source of income is stopped.
2. It has stopped for an indefinite period.
3. Women and children will undoubtedly suffer with loss of men's monies by gambling.

for cheap labour, and Japanese Canadians could be sent there. The next largest group ended up on these sugar beet farms in Alberta and Manitoba. At first, the prospect of farm labour in unknown conditions outside of BC had little appeal for Japanese Canadians who had been used to the milder climate of the west coast, but as room in the BC camps rapidly diminished, the BC Security Commission became more desperate for families to leave the province and resorted to manipulation, especially in the farming towns in the Fraser Valley and in the fishing community at Steveston, both areas with large concentrations of Japanese Canadians. The policy of breaking up families was suspended for those who would go to the sugar beet farms, and this enticement worked, with some 4,000 Japanese Canadians going to the prairies to keep their families together. Many would be horrified by the harsh and primitive living conditions that awaited them on the farms.

Finally, any men who had shown even the slightest "resistance" to the uprooting—some 700—were interned in prisoner of war camps at Petawawa and Angler, in Ontario, many confined in this condition for the duration of the war.

By November 1942, from the government's perspective, the BC Security Commission had been successful in removing "all persons of Japanese racial origin" from the 100-mile "protected area" along the coast. But for those Canadians of Japanese ancestry who had been arbitrarily torn from their homes and scattered all across Canada, the pain of injustice had only just begun.

The Term "Self-Supporting Site"

The term "self-supporting site" was coined by the BC Security Commission to refer to Christina Lake, Bridge River, Minto City, Lillooet, and McGillivray Falls, sites where some Japanese Canadians were allowed to lease farms and resorts and live with fewer restrictions than in the other internment centres.

There is a wide spread belief among Japanese Canadians themselves that the self-supporting sites were only for the richest Japanese Canadians. It is true that those allowed to choose "self-supporting" had to pay for their own transportation and housing materials. By chartering their own trains, they were allowed to take more of their possessions with them, and families could stay together. As well, they could take pride in not having used government assistance to relocate. However, most Japanese Canadians were not offered the option of going to one of these sites, even if they had the economic means.

The term "self-supporting" suggests that other Japanese Canadians were not paying their own expenses. In fact, according to government policy, all Japanese Canadians were required to pay for their own internment. The forced sale of homes, businesses and belongings by the Custodian of Enemy Property was justified as a means of carrying out this policy.

Although the "self-supporting" route has been seen as a privileged one for 1,400 of the 22,000 Japanese Canadians uprooted from the coast, those who relocated in this way did not escape harsh living conditions and discrimination from communities that treated them as "enemy aliens."

CONFISCATION AND SALE OF PROPERTIES

O n January 19, 1943, the Canadian government passed Order in Council PC 469 giving the Custodian of Enemy Property the power to sell, without the owners' consent, properties which had initially been held "in trust." This new measure, compounding the injustice of the mass uprooting, led to the dispossession of Japanese Canadians. With the dismantling of their community, their former social and economic presence on the west coast could now to be erased.

In the spring and summer of 1943, the properties, businesses, houses, and personal effects of all uprooted Japanese Canadians were liquidated by the Custodian of Enemy Property,

and many precious belongings, furniture, pianos, sewing machines, and household goods, were sold or auctioned off at a mere fraction of their value. Trunks full of invaluable family heirlooms, dishes, kimonos, silver, and other objects of personal value—which had been stored away for safekeeping—were auctioned off unopened, many for as low as two dollars a piece. Almost overnight, the intricate social and economic

Interior of a grocery store owned by Japanese Canadians in the Vancouver prewar community, later lost in the mass uprooting. Courtesy of Tameo Kanbara.

Taishodo store, on Powell Street in the heart of "Japanese town" in the Vancouver prewar community. The uprooting destroyed the social and economic base of the Japanese Canadian community. Photo: Vancouver Public Library #11806.

infrastructure of the community was destroyed. Now rootless, dispossessed, and faced with an indefinite period of confinement, Japanese Canadians were no longer able to look forward to returning to their homes on the coast.

The government justified the Custodian's actions as an "efficient" economic policy: the proceeds from the liquidation of the assets of the community would be used to pay for the living expenses of the uprooted Japanese Canadians. Unlike prisoners of war or enemy nationals under the Geneva Convention, Japanese Canadians were forced to pay for their own internment. By this action, the Canadian government had imposed on a group of its own citizens who happened to be of Japanese ancestry, a status lesser than that of nationals from enemy countries.

The politicians and individuals who had been intent on expelling Japanese Canadians from BC, since long before the war, had now finally and successfully used "the politics of racism" to achieve their ends.

PHONE PACIFIC 6131
PLEASE REFER TO
FILE No. 4592
4713

CANADA
DEPARTMENT OF THE SECRETARY OF STATE
OFFICE OF THE CUSTODIAN
——
JAPANESE EVACUATION SECTION

506 ROYAL BANK BLDG.
HASTINGS AND GRANVILLE
VANCOUVER, B.C.

March 9th, 1945.

Dear Sir:

This will acknowledge receipt of your letter of February 2nd, which has been receiving our attention.

Concerning the "kodak camera" Mr. Lord understood you had given him this as an unconditional gift. He later loaned the camera as his own property to an R.C.A.F. officer who has since been killed in action and the camera, no doubt, was destroyed when the plane crashed.

Regarding the articles left at house 48, Phoenix Cannery, which you asked to have shipped, we regret that owing to Government policy we are not permitted to make shipments of such effects, so we are engaged in selling at auction all chattels that have a re-sale value. Some of the goods which we moved from your house 48 have already been sold as also have your A.M.C. frigidaire, and other articles which were vested in Mr. YOSHIDA and sold with his goods, the proceeds credited to his account. We have since credited your account with sale of articles belonging to you.

We must tell you that when removing your goods from house 48 at Phoenix Cannery, we found no trace of an electric clock, medicinal apparatus, electric phonograph, etc., so it is likely these articles were stolen during the epidemic of robberies which were so prevalent in Steveston a year or so ago, as mentioned in previous letters.

Yours truly,

R. B. Mackedie
Protection Department.

RBM:LBM

(above) **Many Japanese Canadians lost personal belongings which were left in their houses, or with friends, when they were uprooted. This letter documents the government's failure to protect their belongings which were left with the Custodian "in trust."** Courtesy of the Japanese Canadian Redress Secretariat.

(above left) **Japanese Canadian farmer in Steveston in the prewar community in front of Dominion Canners BC Limited.** Photo: Japanese Canadian Cultural Centre, Toronto.

Sergeant Masumi Mitsui: 1887-1987

Japanese Canadian volunteers, Tenth Battalion, France, 1917. Front row, left to right: Tsunejiro Kuroda, Kumakichi Oura*. Middle: Masumi Mitsui, Chikara Fujita*, Masaru Nishijima, Toraki Matsumura*, Masajiro

In World War I, Sergeant Masumi Mitsui of the Tenth Battalion, Second Infantry Brigade, First Canadian Division, defended Canada's honour at Vimy Ridge. For his "conspicuous bravery and distinguished conduct," he was awarded the Military Medal.

Park and then to Greenwood, BC and were separated from their children. They decided to send their youngest son Harry, to a school in Lacombe, Alberta. Their two daughters, Lucy and Amy, and another son, Dick, were sent to Strathmore, Alberta by the government. Lucy attended school

settlement or a formal acknowledgement from the federal government. He was one of the last surviving Japanese Canadians who had volunteered for Canada in World War I.

Masumi Mitsui with his daughter, Amy Kuwabara and friends from Maple Ridge, BC at the ceremony on August 2, 1985 to relight the Stanley Park lamp. The memorial was dedicated in 1920 to honour the Japanese Canadian soldiers who fought for Canada in World War I. Photo: Waylen Miki.

Shishido. Back row: Otokichi Onishi*, unknown, Nuinosuke Okawa, Tsunekichi Kitagawa.

*killed in action

Courtesy of Amy Kuwabara; soldiers' names from We Went to War *(Canada's Wings, 1984), frontispiece.*

In World War II, Mitsui, his wife, Sugiko and their five Canadian-born children were labelled "enemy aliens" and forced off their farm in Port Coquitlam, BC. Summoned before a Security Commissioner, Mitsui reached into his pocket, pulled out his World War I medals and threw them on the floor. "What good are these!" he demanded in fury.

Masumi and Sugiko were taken to the livestock pens of Hastings

while Amy and Dick worked on a government farm. Son George remained behind temporarily to look after their poultry farm, but he was soon shipped to Ontario, along with many other younger nisei. The Mitsui family was not re-united until after the war when they settled permanently in Hamilton, Ontario. Sergeant Mitsui died April 22, 1987 at the age of 99, without having witnessed a redress

Japanese Canadian Veterans

Tragically, among those whose rights were abrogated in the mass uprooting were Japanese Canadian veterans of World War I who had fought loyally for Canada. Of the approximately 200 who had volunteered, 54 were killed and most of the others were wounded in battle.

In 1942, a handful of Japanese Canadians already in the Canadian Army were fighting overseas for the same principles that were being violated back home in the uprooting and dispossession of their families, relatives and friends. David Tsubota was interned in a German prisoner of war camp after he was captured at Dieppe, and Minoru Tanaka was killed in action near Calcar, Germany. Both their fathers were Canadian veterans of World War I.

Japanese Canadians in BC who tried to enlist after the declaration of war with Japan in December 1941 were denied the right to serve their country. BC Premier, T. D. Patullo, had vigourously opposed enlistment of Asians in a letter to Prime Minister Mackenzie King, dated September 23, 1940, because then they would demand "they be given the franchise, which we in this province can never tolerate" (Cited in *Democracy Betrayed* [NAJC, 1984]).

Only in January 1945, after the British government asked for Japanese Canadians to join the British army as interpreters for service in southeast Asia, did the Canadian government finally allow them to enlist. While some Japanese Canadians applauded the volunteers' belief that enlisting would confirm their loyalty and belief in Canada, others believed it was foolish to volunteer in view of the injustices suffered by Japanese Canadians at the hands of the Canadian government. Enlisting did not change the status of their families left in Canada, and upon their return, the veterans were still subject to the same restrictions as other Japanese Canadians, including exclusion from the coastal zone.

UPROOTED ONCE MORE

> *"It was a train meant for cows. It was very upsetting. I was three months pregnant and very sick. We were just cleared out. I swore I'd never come back to British Columbia. But I did, and I still think Canada's the freest country in the world. When the Olympic Games were on and the Japanese flag was flown, I felt nothing. When I saw the Maple Leaf, I got tears in my eyes."*
>
> *Mary Oike, from "The Wound That Hasn't Healed," by Tim Harper,* The Toronto Star, *February 22, 1987.*

> *"Let our slogan be for British Columbia: 'No Japs from the Rockies to the seas.'"*
>
> *Ian Alistair Mackenzie, MP, from his nomination speech, September 18, 1944, from* Democracy Betrayed *(NAJC, 1984).*

Apologists for the government's actions pointed to the war hysteria on the west coast and argued that the fear of sabotage by Japanese Canadians—though unfounded—was nevertheless a concern that had to be addressed. They also added that the wartime atmosphere was so tense with antagonism towards Japanese Canadians, that the mass uprooting was a way of protecting them from racial violence. Such an "explanation" was actively promoted by the government of the day, and continued in the minds of many Canadians until only recently.

The truth is that Japanese Canadians had been swept up in the politically motivated machinery of racist attitudes which were endorsed and legalized by government policies. Instead of protecting the freedom of Japanese Canadians, and using the full force of the law to do so, it was the government itself which established the racist principle of "blaming the victim" to justify the destruction of the Japanese Canadian community.

In August 1944, while the rights of Japanese Canadians were still restricted, Prime Minister Mackenzie King declared in the House of Commons:

> It is a fact no person of Japanese race born in Canada has been charged with any act of sabotage or disloyalty during the years of war. (*Debates,* House of Commons, August 4, 1944)

By August 1944, the imagined threat to national security was no longer an issue for King, and no

DEPARTMENT OF LABOUR

CANADA

NOTICE

TO ALL PERSONS OF JAPANESE RACIAL ORIGIN

HAVING REFERENCE TO MAKING APPLICATION FOR VOLUNTARY REPATRIATION TO JAPAN

The Minister of Labour has been authorized by the Government of Canada to make known the following decisions made with respect to persons of Japanese ancestry, now resident in Canada, who make voluntary application to go to Japan after the war, or sooner where this can be arranged:

1. The net proceeds realized from the disposition of their property, real and personal, in Canada, and standing to their credit at time of repatriation, will be secured to them and may be transferred by them to Japan upon repatriation following the close of the war.

2. In the case of persons sent to Japan under any agreement for exchange of Nationals between Canada and Japan before the close of war, under which agreement the amount of personal property and funds carried by the repatriates is limited, the Custodian of Enemy Alien Property will be authorized, on the advice of the Department of External Affairs, to provide such Japanese repatriates with receipts showing the property left behind in Canada, or net proceeds of same if sold, with a view to their being permitted to secure possession of their property or the net proceeds thereof after the end of hostilities.

3. Free passage will be guaranteed by the Canadian Government to all repatriates being sent to Japan, and all their dependents who accompany them, and including free transportation of such of their personal property as they may take with them.

The above assurances will apply to such persons as have already made written application in satisfactory form to the Government of Canada to go to Japan, or who make written application hereafter for that purpose to the Government of Canada within the period of time fixed by the Commissioner of Japanese Placement for the completion and filing of applications.

These assurances do not apply to persons of the Japanese race repatriated on other than a voluntary basis.

Dated at Ottawa this 13th day of February, 1945.

HUMPHREY MITCHELL
Minister of Labour.

The so-called "repatriation" order that would lead to the exiling of some 4,000 Japanese Canadians to Japan.

acts of sabotage or disloyalty by Japanese Canadians had occurred. And yet, despite this recognition, he did not allow them to return to the coast. In the wake of this unequivocal acknowledgement by the Prime Minister in 1944, the subsequent actions of the Canadian government clearly showed that the Japanese Canadian community had not been uprooted under the War Measures Act for the sake of

"1. Do we have free choice
   of living space?
2. Do we have free choice
   of occupation?
3. Will our children have
   equal education?
4. Do we have any
   security after we move
   into the new place?...
5. If you send us to the
   most anti-Japanese locality, if anything
   happens to me or my
   family, who's going to be
   responsible? The government, or are we just out
   of luck?
"Pickersgill's answer, which
Nihei recalled as if it were
yesterday, was: 'If you have
those worries, sign it (the
repatriation form), and
your worries are all gone.'"

*Questions posed in 1945 by issei John
Nihei to T.B. Pickersgill, Commissioner
of Japanese Placement, about moving
east of the Rockies; cited in* Redress for
Japanese Canadians: A Community
Forum *(JCCA Redress Committee,
1984).*

48

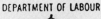

CANADA

NOTICE

To All Persons of Japanese Racial Origin Now Resident in British Columbia

1. Japanese Nationals and others of Japanese racial origin who will be returning to Japan, have been informed by notice issued on the authority of the Honourable Minister of Labour, that provision has been made for their return and for the filing of an application for such return. Conditions in regard to property and transportation have been made public.

2. Japanese Canadians who want to remain in Canada should now re-establish themselves East of the Rockies as the best evidence of their intentions to co-operate with the Government policy of dispersal.

3. Failure to accept employment east of the Rockies may be regarded at a later date as lack of co-operation with the Canadian Government in carrying out its policy of dispersal.

4. Several thousand Japanese have already re-established themselves satisfactorily east of the Rockies.

5. Those who do not take advantage of present opportunities for employment and settlement outside British Columbia at this time, while employment opportunities are favourable, will find conditions of employment and settlement considerably more difficult at a later date and may seriously prejudice their own future by delay.

6. To assist those who want to re-establish themselves in Canada, the Japanese Division Placement Offices and the Employment and Selective Service Offices, with the assistance of local Advisory Committees, are making special efforts this Spring to open up suitable employment opportunities across Canada in various lines of endeavour, and in areas where prospects of suitable employment are best.

7. The Department will also provide free transportation to Eastern Canada for members of a family and their effects, a sustenance allowance to be used while in transit, and a placement allowance based in amount on the size of the family.

T. B. PICKERSGILL,
COMMISSIONER OF JAPANESE PLACEMENT

Vancouver, B.C.
March 12th, 1945.

national security. The wartime dispersal was simply the first phase in the government's plan to permanently erase the presence of the Japanese Canadian community on the BC coast for reasons other than national security.

In the spring of 1945—while Japanese Americans were free to return to the coast—Japanese Canadians were about to undergo another uprooting. This second uprooting was designed as the "final solution" to the so-called "Japanese problem" in Canada.

By then, with the war all but over, Japanese Canadians had been interned for three years. Their former lives had been obliterated, their assets depleted, and they were suffering from severe demoralization. It was in this climate of anguish and disbelief that they were approached by representatives from the Department of Labour with the government's double-edged scheme to solve the problem of their rootlessness. Two simultaneous policies were announced: "dispersal" and "repatriation." Japanese Canadians were now required to "choose" between "dispersal" east of the Rockies, or "repatriation" to Japan. The government's pernicious term "repatriation" was the euphemism for what was, in actuality, a forced exile; the "patria" or country of birth for the majority of these citizens was Canada, so they could not, in this sense, be "repatriated" to Japan.

A cruel irony awaited many Japanese Canadians who "chose" to go to Japan. As a defeated country, Japan may have been forced by Canada to accept them, but there was no obligation on Japan to treat them as their own. The Canadian-born nisei thus found themselves categorized, in Japan, as "aliens." They had become totally rootless exiles.

The purpose behind the either/or options—"dispersal" versus "repatriation"—was, of course,

This "Certificate for Registration of Alien" was an identification card for a Japanese Canadian who was treated as an "enemy alien" in Canada, and exiled under the "repatriation" program. Ironically, when she landed in Japan, as a Canadian-born person, she was considered a Canadian citizen and thus an "alien" in Japan. On the card her name is written in katakana, a syllabic script used for foreign names and words. Japanese names are normally written using ideogrammic characters called kanji. Courtesy of Irene (Kato) Tsuyuki.

"You are not obliged to report to the RCMPolice unless you are planning to go to Japan after the cessation of hostilities and wish to take advantage of the assistance provided by the Government to all those making voluntary applications.

"This assured assistance from the Government, as outlined in the ["repatriation"] notice, will mean to many who desire repatriation, relief from unnecessary anxiety and it will allow them to plan for their future, and that of their children, along economic, social, and cultural lines which they fear may be denied them were they to remain in Canada."

T.B. Pickersgill, Commissioner for the BC Security Commission, in a form letter to Japanese Canadians, this one dated March 28, 1945.

Uprooting of Japanese Americans: with a soldier in a truck leaving Bainbridge Island, Washington, are Seijiro Nakamura, Ruth Nakamura, Archie Nakamura, Yuki Nakamura, **Pastor Kihachi Hirakawa, and Jane Nakamura.** *Photo: Library of Congress LC-USZ62-61122; names from* Coming Home *(Japanese American Citizens League, 1988), p. 38.*

to force Japanese Canadians out of BC permanently, which in effect would prevent them from rebuilding their community on the coast. They were not permitted the third option, to remain in BC; nor were their family members, trapped in Japan by the war, permitted to come back to Canada. The coercive thrust of these policies was implicit in the bureaucratic language of the "dispersal" notice: refusal to relocate east of the Rockies would be taken as evidence of disloyalty.

Japanese Canadians were aware that resistance to the parameters of this limited "choice" would be judged an act of disloyalty, which could very well result in deportation later. That was their interpretation of the warning in the government's "dispersal" order that those who did not leave BC "may seriously prejudice their own future by delay." Their fears were further reinforced by Prime Minister King's announcement proposing the "establishment of a quasi-judicial commission to examine the background, loyalties and attitudes of all persons of Japanese race in Canada to ascertain those who are not fit persons to be allowed to remain here" (*Debates,* House of Commons, August 4, 1944).

In August 1944, in his House of Commons speech declaring the innocence of Japanese Canadians, Prime Minister King went on to justify his government's dispersal policy:

> The sound policy and the best policy for the Japanese Canadians themselves is to distribute their numbers as widely as possible throughout the country where they will not create feelings of racial hostility. (*Debates,* House of Commons, August 4, 1944)

By positing a rationale for the dispersal policy, Prime Minister King exposed the nature of the

Japanese American Internment

On February 19, 1942, US President Roosevelt issued Executive Order 9066, authorizing the incarceration of 120,000 Japanese Americans living on the west coast. As in Canada, the American decision was a political one. The FBI had advised that mass uprooting was not necessary. Nor did the most senior military officials believe that individuals of Japanese ancestry constituted a security risk. Japanese Americans were drafted and allowed to enlist in the American armed forces. In Hawaii, persons of Japanese ancestry continued their employment at the Pearl Harbor US Naval base even after the Japanese bombing, and Japanese Hawaiians who made up a third of the population were not uprooted.

The coastal Japanese Americans were sent to concentration camps, fenced with barbed wire and guarded by armed soldiers. Treated as prisoners of war, they did not have to use their savings to house and feed themselves. Although their property, registered in the name of their American-born children, was protected from confiscation by the US Constitution, many sold in panic, and untended businesses, homes and farms depreciated or were looted. Unlike Canadian policies intended to permanently destroy the Japanese Canadian coastal communities, US policies did not force Japanese Americans to move east or be exiled to Japan after the war.

CONSTITUTIONAL VICTORY

In December 1944, James Purcell, a San Francisco attorney, successfully filed a habeas corpus petition in the famous Mitsuye Endo case, and challenged her incarceration on the grounds that the US Constitution guarantees freedom of movement for all Americans. The US Supreme Court agreed that an American could not be detained any longer than necessary to determine loyalty, nor could loyal Japanese Americans be excluded from any part of the USA open to other Americans. In January 1945, before Japan's surrender, Japanese Americans began returning to the coast. It wasn't until April 1, 1949 that Japanese Canadians were allowed to enter the 100-mile coastal zone.

A Comparison Between the Japanese Canadian and the Japanese American Experiences:

CANADA	USA
- civilian police directed uprooting	- army directed uprooting
- 22,000 uprooted from 100-mile coastal zone	- 120,000 uprooted from west coast
- government seized and sold land and personal property	- panic sales, looting, depreciation, but no government sale of property because of constitutional protections
- ghost towns used for internment	- barbed wire and armed guards in internment camps
- internees paid for food, clothes and improvements in basic housing from savings and proceeds of property sales	- housing and food provided
- not allowed to join armed forces until January 1945, and then only as translators	- drafted and allowed to enlist
- no legislated protection of human rights even for Canadian-born	- Constitution provided American citizens could not be held without just cause
- allowed to return to the coast April 1, 1949	- American citizens began returning to the coast in January 1945
- Bird Commission paid $1.2 million for property losses	- $37 million paid, despite no government seizure and sale of property, which was only one-tenth of the losses claimed
- breakup of families	- incarceration in family groups
- policy of exile to Japan and dispersal eastward, continuing after World War II, until March 31, 1949	- no similar policy of exile and dispersal either during or after World War II

Fighting for the Franchise

Japanese Canadians, whether naturalized or Canadian-born nisei, were denied the vote in BC, which effectively meant they could not vote federally or municipally because the provincial voters' list was used for federal elections. Because they were not on the voters' list, Japanese Canadians were also barred from numerous professions, including law and pharmacy, and from holding municipal office. During World War I, some Japanese Canadians enlisted to fight for Canada in an attempt to win the franchise; after years of lobbying, the surviving veterans were given the vote in 1931. However, the right to vote did not extend to their wives or children.

In 1936 the Japanese Canadian Citizens' League (JCCL) was formed by nisei seeking full rights of citizenship, including the franchise. They hired a lawyer to prepare a brief, and the four delegates made a presentation to the Special Committee on Elections and Franchise Acts in Ottawa to secure the right to vote for Japanese Canadians in BC, despite the province's voting restrictions.

Elsewhere in Canada, Japanese Canadians had been allowed to vote provincially and federally, so it appeared that the forced dispersal eastward might result in at least one benefit. That hope was dashed when, in 1944, the federal government passed a new law denying the vote to those who were not eligible to vote in the previous election. This law was specifically intended to apply to those Japanese Canadians, now outside of BC, who had previously been disenfranchised as BC residents. It was not until 1949 that all Japanese Canadians enjoyed the basic democratic right to vote.

Delegation to Ottawa in 1936. Left to right: Samuel I. Hayakawa, Minoru Kobayashi, Hide (Hyodo) Shimizu, Edward Banno.
Photo: Japanese Canadian Cultural Centre, Toronto.

government's victimization of Japanese Canadians. Rather than addressing the question of national security, the government's alleged reason for the euphemistic "evacuation," he dwelt on their visibility as a group and blamed the hostility towards them on the fact of their being "visible."

Japanese Canadians, King reasoned, became victims because of their visible racial ancestry. Adopting the language of racism, he then reinforced their victimization by explaining that the dispersal policy was designed for their benefit. Once dispersed, and so not visible as a group—one that might act together with the political power a community implies—they would no longer be in a position to "create feelings of racial hostility." They would now be politically isolated, and hence powerless individuals without a constituency. King assumed without question that racism existed in Canada, but instead of blaming its source, the white racists in BC, he blamed its victims, Japanese Canadians. By reasoning as he did, King endorsed a policy of cultural genocide and disguised it as benign paternalism. Japanese Canadians themselves were forced to bear the blame for the injustices inflicted on them. The effects of this condition would shape their lives in the years ahead.

In the heat of the moment, some 10,000 Japanese Canadians signed up for expulsion to Japan. Many feared the forced dispersal east from BC: How would they survive in what appeared to be hostile conditions east of the Rockies? Others had lost faith in Canadian democracy and began to think they might be better off in Japan. The camps were rife with conflicting attitudes: Why stay in a country that does not respect basic human rights?

As Canadians, though, what other country did they have? Still others were led to believe by the RCMP that they were responding to a survey, and that they could change their minds later. So as Japanese Americans returned to their homes and businesses, which had not been confiscated and liquidated, Japanese Canadians were preparing for the ultimate injustice: deportation from their own country.

Thousands who had signed for "repatriation," either out of fear, or lack of a clear understanding of their alternatives, soon changed their minds. The government, nevertheless, made moves in the fall of 1945 to hold them to their coerced decisions, and to deport them. By then, however, the war was over and Canadians in general were finally becoming aware of the extent of injustices inflicted on a group of fellow Canadians who had not committed any crime—who had not even been charged with any crime!—but who faced deportation and loss of citizenship simply on the basis of their racial ancestry. The very horror of injustices and racism that the democratic countries, including Canada, had been fighting since 1939, was apparently flourishing in one of those democratic countries—Canada.

In June 1945, the Co-operative Committee on Japanese Canadians was formed in support of Japanese Canadians who faced both deportation and the continued abrogation of their rights as Canadian citizens. Working closely with the recently formed nisei organization, the Japanese Canadian Committee for Democracy, the Co-operative Committee quickly grew into a broad-based national coalition of over thirty organizations, including labour and church groups, civil liberties and professional associations, and many Canadians who expressed outrage at the mistreatment of fellow citizens by their own

Photo: National Archives of Canada C57252.

"*I had the queerest sensation of living in some fantastic dream as the train slowly moved out of the station. All along the tracks, wherever they could, crowds of nihonjin lined up to wave good-bye to those going to work camps, to Schreiber and to beet fields, ghost towns and other places. They waved to us and we waved to them, whoever they were. Some we knew, some we didn't, but weren't we all in the same boat—forced to move out of the restricted area?*"

Muriel Kitagawa, *from* This Is My Own (Talonbooks, 1985), p. 1.

53

Haruko Kobayakawa: 1902-1989

Haruko Kobayakawa at a community meeting, October 1988.
Photo: Cassandra Kobayashi.

Late in life, when other seniors of her generation were withdrawing from public affairs, Haruko Kobayakawa became an active member of the Greater Vancouver Japanese Canadian Citizens' Association, from 1984 to the time of her death. Through her dedication to the principle of justice and her fluency in Japanese, she attracted many issei of her generation to the redress movement.

A pioneer issei who came to Canada in 1921, Haruko spent the early years of her marriage to Masao Kobayakawa, a Canadian-born nisei, in Courtenay on Vancouver Island where she became the first teacher of Japanese in that community.

While visiting Japan in 1941 she was unfortunately trapped there, and consequently separated from her uprooted husband in Ontario, until October 1948. She rejoined him in Toronto and resettled there until the 1970s when she returned, a widow, to the west coast. Like other Japanese Canadians, Haruko and her husband had had their home on Vancouver Island confiscated and sold without their consent.

In an interview for the Vancouver JCCA *Bulletin*, October 1987, Haruko recalled the years of exile and tragedy in Japan. Many of her relatives were killed in the bombing of Hiroshima. She herself was there just the day before and nearly stayed for a visit. Though saved from certain death, she witnessed the destruction: "...I heard a terrible BANG. I rushed outside and in the direction of Hiroshima City a big mushroom-like cloud hung overhead. Of course at that time we didn't know that it was the atomic bomb. Then a black rain fell and many people died just by breathing in the air."

She was one of the first issei to join the redress movement. "Many young people were working on our behalf," she explained, "so even though I am old, I couldn't sit back and let them do everything...I felt that as an issei I should be involved too. I can't help much but I hope I can give encouragement by my presence."

Haruko so passionately believed in her community's dream of justice that she dedicated the final years of her life to its fulfillment, sharing her late husband's reaction to the uprooting: "He always used to say he was a native-born Canadian and had looked upon Canada as his homeland but even at that he was treated like a man who, after having his legs and arms cut off, was thrown out into the freezing snow. He felt helpless. He often talked about that and what a terrible injustice it was."

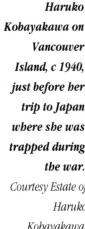

Haruko Kobayakawa on Vancouver Island, c 1940, just before her trip to Japan where she was trapped during the war.
Courtesy Estate of Haruko Kobayakawa.

government. They disseminated educational materials, lobbied the government to change its position on deportation, and called for the lifting of restrictions on Japanese Canadians.

Despite the public opposition, and perhaps with a sense of defiance, the government went ahead and passed the deportation orders in council in December 1945. In response, the Co-operative Committee challenged the Minister of Justice, Louis St. Laurent, to refer the issue to the Supreme Court of Canada for a ruling. St. Laurent agreed, believing that the government's position under the War Measures Act would be upheld.

In February 1946, the Supreme Court of Canada did indeed rule that the government had the legal right, under the War Measures Act, to deport Japanese Canadians, but with one exception: the wives and dependent children who had not signed for "repatriation" were exempt. This renewed prospect of the government breaking up families, especially in the face of growing sympathy and support for Japanese Canadians, led Prime Minister Mackenzie King to call off the deportation orders—even after the Privy Council later upheld the government's power to exile unwilling dependents.

Tragically, despite the successful public challenge to deportation in 1946, by then some 4,000 individuals had already left Canada, including 2,000 who were Canadian-born, of which one-third were dependent children under the age of 16.

Japanese Canadians finally received the right to the federal vote in June 1948 (effective April 1949). They received the right to the BC vote in March 1949. On April 1, 1949, the last restriction imposed on them was lifted, and they were finally free to return to the west coast, four years after the end of World War II.

But by 1949, it was too late for reconstruction. The community they had known had been obliterated—its very foundations had disappeared. Most had no choice but to dig in where they had been re-settled, and begin rebuilding their lives in the places to which they had been dispersed.

Japanese Canadians who were trapped in Japan were considered enemies of Canada. Half the rent for the Kobayakawas' house was seized by the Custodian on this basis. Courtesy Estate of Haruko Kobayakawa.

CANADA
DEPARTMENT OF THE SECRETARY OF STATE
OFFICE OF THE CUSTODIAN
—
JAPANESE EVACUATION SECTION

PHONE PACIFIC 6131
PLEASE REFER TO
FILE NO. 4952.

506 ROYAL BANK BLDG.,
HASTINGS AND GRANVILLE
VANCOUVER, B.C.

December 17th, 1943.

Mr. Masao KOBAYAKAWA,
Registration No. 06228,
c/o Spadoni Bros.,
Schreiber, Ontario.

Dear Sir:,

We are in receipt of your letter of the 7th instant enquiring whether you can claim the rent derived from the Courtenay property owned jointly by yourself and your wife.

Your wife being resident in Japan creates a 50% Enemy interest in this property and you are therefore entitled to half the net revenue only. At the present time this 50% amounts to $96.44, less $3.50 (claim passed and paid on your behalf).

The only other claim registered against you having been withdrawn the proceeds from sale of your speed boat ($150.00) has been freed and added to the above net balance ($92.94) makes a total balance of $242.94 available to you in your account.

Yours truly,

R. G. Bell,
Administration Department.

55

SEEKING COMPENSATION IN THE 1940s

Even as late as 1947, two years after the war, Japanese Canadians had to apply for a license to purchase property.
Courtesy of Harry (Hiroshi) Yonekura.

LICENSE

FOR A PERSON OF THE JAPANESE RACE
TO ACQUIRE REAL PROPERTY IN CANADA

Pursuant to the provisions of Order in Council P.C. 946 of February 5, 1943, as amended by Order in Council P.C. 5973 of September 14, 1945, the Minister of Labour does hereby grant to

HIROSHI YONEKURA of TORONTO, Ontario,

(Reg. No. 03344)

a License to acquire and hold the following real property, namely:

ALL AND SINGULAR Lot No.33 as registered in the Toronto Registry Office on Plan No.M--8, for the City of Toronto, County of York, Province of Ontario; and more commonly known as No.65 Brooklyn Avenue, Toronto, Ontario.

Dated at Ottawa, Canada, this 13th day of Jan'y. 1947

Minister of Labour

The first attempt by Japanese Canadians to seek compensation for the injustices they suffered was launched in the 1940s. In Toronto, as early as 1943, a handful of nisei formed the Japanese Canadian Committee for Democracy, a group that wanted to continue the struggle by the community—begun in the 1930s—to achieve full citizenship rights and to assess the economic losses resulting from the mass uprooting. Later, in 1947, this organization was eclipsed through the formation of a national organization, the National Japanese Canadian Citizens' Association (NJCCA), which would become the National Association of Japanese Canadians (NAJC) in 1980. At the time, the NJCCA was made up of five provincial chapters: Quebec, Ontario, Manitoba, Alberta, and British Columbia. The long-term objective of the NJCCA was to become the voice of Japanese Canadians across Canada in their struggle for the franchise; the immediate goal was to press for compensation through the government's proposed Royal Commission to investigate losses, headed by Justice Henry Bird of BC. When the Bird Commission hearings got underway, the NJCCA chapters helped individuals fill in their claim forms.

The Bearer, whose photograph and specimen of signature appear hereon, has been duly registered in compliance with the provisions of Order-in-Council P. C. 117.

Vancouver
(Date) February 15, 1946.

CANADIAN BORG 117

Issuing Officer _____ R.C.M.P.

The violation of rights continued until April 1, 1949. Even those Japanese Canadians who had been residing outside the 100-mile "protected area" in 1942 were still required to register after the war was over. Susan Kobayashi, born and raised in the Okanagan, had to register when she turned 16 in 1946. *Courtesy of Susan (Kobayashi) Hidaka.*

Some 500 Japanese Canadians marched on Ottawa in April 1988 to call on the government to negotiate a redress settlement with the NAJC. *Photo: Gordon King.*

Community interest in the redress issue was rekindled in 1984 during the early phase of the NAJC's campaign. In the first public meeting on redress in Vancouver over 500 people packed the old Japanese Language School on Alexander Street. *Photo: Ian Lindsay, Vancouver Sun.*

" *We matured during the evacuation. We realized what was behind all of this. You start thinking, by God, I'm a Canadian and why the hell are they doing this to us.* "

A statement made in a seminar, "The Impact of the Uprooting," NAJC Conference, Vancouver, May 1987; from Spirit of Redress *(JC Publications, 1989), p. 94.*

57

Objections to the Bird Commission's Waiver

Not all Japanese Canadians were willing to accept the Bird Commission's rulings. Roger Obata recalled, "The final straw that broke the camel's back, as far as I'm concerned, was when the Commission asked us to sign a waiver. Kunio Hidaka and I threw up our hands in disgust and said to the Co-operative Committee on Japanese Canadians, if you people want to go along with the Bird Commission's ruling on this waiver, you go ahead, but as far as we're concerned there's more unfinished business to be dealt with, but if we sign this waiver it's finished once and for all. This is why we objected" (From an unpublished personal interview with Roy Miki, October 29-30, 1985).

The fact that the Bird Commission was seen by some Japanese Canadians as a further injustice left the way open for future redress.

Japanese Canadians were bitterly disappointed by the Bird Commission's terms of reference which were deliberately restricted to economic losses from the sale of properties in the care of the Custodian of Enemy Property. The Commission could not raise the issue of compensation for civil rights violation, nor could it question the legitimacy of the decision to liquidate properties that the Custodian was supposed to hold "in trust." Other damages, such as loss of income, disruption of education, emotional and psychological traumas, were also deliberately excluded. The jurisdiction of the Commission was restricted to the question of administering the policy which had dispossessed Japanese Canadians, not the policy itself.

As the hearings began, Justice Bird considered only those losses related to property—and even more narrowly, to those losses calculated from the difference between the sale price set by the Custodian of Enemy Property, and the fair market value of that property at the time of sale. The losses were even more unfairly diminished because many properties deteriorated once vacated, and prices were depressed during the war. To make matters worse for the claimants, the onus was on the property owner to prove the "market" value. Even within these constricted parameters, the Commission eventually decided that proceeding with individual cases was too time-consuming, and ended up treating losses in broad general categories. For the Japanese Canadians who had suffered enormous economic and personal losses, the terms of reference and the methods used for the Commission were not adequate to ensure fair compensation. After Justice Bird's report was filed in 1950, only $1.2 million was paid to those individuals who had submitted claims—and many Japanese Canadians had not—from which they had to deduct their legal fees.

The Bird Commission effectively quelled further protests and challenges to the government's wartime policies and actions. As a political tool, it worked well to diffuse public opinion and to close the door on negotiations towards a just and honourable resolution to the injustices. A cloak of silence fell over the Japanese Canadian community in the 1950s. Dispersed from BC, they quietly rebuilt new lives in scattered places all over Canada.

"...I find your action to be morally and politically reprehensible. At the time the property was registered with you it was clearly understood that it was 'a protective measure only.'
"...I raise an additional objection regarding the price. The sale price of two hundred and eighty-seven dollars ($287.00) is altogether inadequate. Prior to our evacuation, we refused offers of seventeen and eighteen hundred dollars. Under no circumstance can your reported price be considered fair and reasonable."

From a letter, November 15, 1946, from Kunio Hidaka to the Custodian returning a cheque for the sale of his property. Courtesy of Susan Hidaka.

Kunio Hidaka in Ocean Falls, in 1941, just before the uprooting. He was active in the National Japanese Canadian Citizens' Association (NJCCA) during the Bird Commission hearings, and joined the redress struggle in the 1980s. Kunio was an important part of the Toronto Japanese Canadian community that rallied behind the NAJC. He died suddenly and unexpectedly during the campaign. *Courtesy of Susan Hidaka.*

" *With the use of the government's own documents,* The Politics of Racism *seeks to strip away the mask of wartime rhetoric and examine from the perspective of federal government policy the seven years in which Japanese Canadians were exiled in their own country. It is the story of how the government came to set its harsh policies. It traces the evolution of those policies from their birth in the rhetoric of British Columbia politicians, through their maturation in the wartime government of William Lyon Mackenzie King, to their implementation under the all-powerful War Measures Act—despite opposition by Canada's leading military and police officers, and in one case, by Parliament itself.* "

Ann Sunahara, from the Introduction, p. 3.

It was not until the mid-1970s that the thirty-year ban on access to World War II government files was lifted and researchers could begin to reassess the government's wartime actions. Historian Ann Gomer Sunahara paved the way for a re-examination of the uprooting by drawing on the newly available documents in the National Archives of Canada. Her study, *The Politics of Racism* (Lorimer, 1981), provided irrefutable proof that the uprooting of Japanese Canadians was a political, and not a security measure. There, in the dusty archives, she

Ann Sunahara, author of The Politics of Racism, speaking on Japanese Canadian redress at the NAJC National Conference, May 1987, Vancouver. *Photo: Connie Kadota.*

unearthed evidence in the black-and-white of memos and reports, stating clearly and unequivocally, that the military advisors of the day, and the RCMP, had not viewed the Japanese Canadian community on the west coast as a threat to national security. It had been the influential Ian Mackenzie, MP for Vancouver Centre, and adviser to Prime Minister Mackenzie King on the so-called

Photo: *Japanese Canadian Cultural Centre, Toronto.*

"Japanese problem," who had pressed for the mass uprooting of Japanese Canadians as a political means of accommodating the powerful pressure from racist politicians and individuals in BC.

Coincidental with this new evidence, 1977 witnessed a resurgence of pride and self-awareness among Japanese Canadians, when local communities across Canada celebrated the 100-year anniversary of the first Japanese immigrant, Manzo Nagano, settling in Canada.

The documents, and the renewed interest in their Canadian past, gave Japanese Canadians the confidence and courage to tell their story—the inside story of the uprooting through the eyes of those who had been directly affected. The silence had been broken, and the time was ripe for a new redress movement to begin.

" A sense of incompleteness gnaws at me. I need to feel right about my country. I need this to happen while I am still around to appreciate it. What would finally ease the bitter memories and deep hurts that simmer inside me is for the government in Ottawa to take the high road in producing a Redress settlement. It should not only satisfy Japanese Canadians but also assure all Canadians that, despite temporary aberrations, our country guarantees that the rights and privileges of citizenship cannot be taken away, for whatever reason. "

Frank Moritsugu, World War II veteran, Winnipeg Free Press, *August 2, 1987; quoted in* Justice in Our Time *(NAJC, 1988).*

61

THE REDRESS MOVEMENT

SEEKING REDRESS—BEGINNINGS

Canadian-born children Yukiko and Sakon (Don) Sato at the Slocan City train station in 1946, leaving for Japan. Don was born in Slocan two years before—and remained in Japan until 1960 when he and his sister returned.
Photo: Japanese Canadian Centennial Project.

The historic Redress Agreement signed by the NAJC and the federal government on September 22, 1988, brought to a stunning climax over a decade of work by the Japanese Canadian community. The story of the movement to seek redress for the injustices of the 1940s is one of the most important in the history of democratic community action in Canada.

It was in 1977 that the National Japanese Canadian Citizens' Association (re-named the National Association of Japanese Canadians in 1980), the national organization which had been formed in 1947 to represent Japanese Canadians, first established a Reparations Committee to investigate the question of redress. Over the next three years, a number of meetings were held in Toronto where the Committee was based, and a preliminary survey was conducted, but because of a lack of urgency and interest, little was done to publicize the issue in the grass-roots Japanese Canadian communities across Canada.

Media interest in Japanese Canadian redress was finally sparked in 1980, when the US Congress established the Commission on Wartime Relocation and Internment of Civilians, to assess the wartime uprooting and incarceration of Japanese Americans. The moving testimony, made to this committee by many Japanese Americans, attracted public sympathy, and Canadian journalists who began investigating the internment of Japanese Canadians were surprised to learn that the violations and losses to persons of Japanese ancestry had been even more severe in Canada than in the United States of America.

In February 1983, the US Commission submitted its report, *Personal Justice Denied*, recommending a public "apology" and compensation of $20,000

" *Why bring up what is past?*
• *It is crucial to the integrity of our community that we seek a resolution to the unfinished business of the war years. Until we speak out and demand justice for the wrongs done to us, the hurt and damage of those years can never truly be past.*
• *Once this past is resolved, we will be free to build a stronger and healthier community.*
• *Canadians need education about the history and consequences of racism. It is important to fight racism instead of hiding from it.* "

From the pamphlet "Redress for Japanese Canadians," published by the Japanese Canadian Centennial Project, Redress Committee, January 1982.

The Japanese Canadian Centennial Project (JCCP) Redress Committee

The Japanese Canadian Centennial Project (JCCP) was formed in Vancouver by a group of sansei, younger nisei, and new immigrants, who mounted a photo history of Japanese Canadians, "A Dream of Riches: Japanese Canadians, 1877-1977," as a national project for the Japanese Canadian Centennial. The exhibit opened in Ottawa in 1977 and eventually toured throughout Canada and Japan, and in its book form, helped stimulate renewed interest in Japanese Canadian history and identity.

In early 1981, the nucleus of the JCCP, joined by other concerned Japanese Canadians, created the JCCP Redress Committee. The objective of this group was to educate Japanese Canadians and other Canadians on the wartime injustices and to advocate redress. A JCCP Redress Committee pamphlet, published in 1982, attracted the attention of the news media, especially in light of the US Congressional Commission hearings on redress taking place for Japanese Americans.

The JCCP Redress Committee sponsored two major community forums on redress in 1982, and its members were to appear in numerous interviews during 1982-83, including *The New York Times, The L.A. Times,* and the CBC television's *The Journal.* Their early work, in the Vancouver area particularly, introduced many Japanese Canadians to the issue of redress.

During the active period of their work, some 25-30 sansei and nisei took part in the JCCP Redress Committee.

The Sodan-Kai

The Sodan-Kai (translated "study group") was formed in Toronto by a group of sansei and nisei in late 1982 to promote awareness of redress. Concerned that the issue was in danger of being resolved without grass-roots community participation, they were to organize a number of large public meetings where information was disseminated and various points of view were heard.

The Sodan-Kai saw themselves as community facilitators, so they did not advocate a position on redress. They wished to contribute to the democratic process through open discussion, community meetings, educational activities, writing, and listening, hoping this process would lead to consensus and unity before any proposal was put to the Canadian government.

The group gained prominence in the Toronto area in 1983 because of their resistance to George Imai, then Chair of the NAJC's National Redress Committee, who wanted to resolve the issue quickly through a community fund without meaningful debate and discussion on what form redress should take. They organized

three influential community meetings in 1983, on May 15, July 23, and October 23. It was through their efforts that Japanese Canadians in the Toronto area were able to express their views in favour of individual compensation, a position Imai opposed.

At the October community meeting, a vote on forms of compensation was taken, and of the 94 who voted, 50 favoured individual compensation, 20 favoured group compensation, and 24 favoured a combination of individual and group compensation. This breakdown was later found comparable to the results of the NAJC's Redress Questionnaire distributed in the spring of 1986.

The Sodan-Kai was also responsible for the short-lived but valuable publication *RedressNews*, beginning in October 1983. At the time, while the two community papers, the *New Canadian* and the *Canada Times,* were publishing hostile and misinformed articles on the NAJC, this newsletter was an important vehicle for publishing up-to-date redress news and for involving Toronto Japanese Canadians in the movement.

HAVE YOU HAD YOUR SAY?

A J.C. POSITION ON REDRESS WILL BE PRESENTED TO THE GOVERNMENT THE FALL OF 1983

SPEAKERS:

MIN YASUI · CHAIRMAN OF J.A.C.L. REDRESS COMMITTEE

GEORGE IMAI · NATIONAL REDRESS COMMITTEE, N.A.J.C. - TORONTO

GORDON KADOTA · PRESIDENT, N.A.J.C. - VANCOUVER

JOY KOGAWA · READING FROM 'OBASAN'

PLACE: JAPANESE CANADIAN CULTURAL CENTRE 123 WYNFORD DRIVE DON MILLS, ONTARIO M3C 2S2 441-2345

DATE: SUNDAY, MAY 15, 1983

TIME: 2.30 - 4.30 P.M.

· SPONSORED BY: **SODAN KAI** ·

THIS MEETING ENDORSED BY THE TORONTO CHAPTER OF THE J.C.C.A.

MEETING IN JAPANESE AND ENGLISH

Poster for a community meeting in Toronto, on May 15, 1983, organized by the Sodan-Kai.

for each uprooted Japanese American. The news of substantial redress for Japanese American individuals generated a burst of public curiosity in the wartime history of Japanese Canadians. Could Japanese Canadians seek a similar redress settlement based on the violation of their rights during the 1940s? The question stimulated discussion in the community, but soon created conflicts in the NAJC. In early 1983, the NAJC Reparations Committee, re-named the National Redress Committee and chaired by George Imai in Toronto, had already begun advocating a redress package consisting of an acknowledgement of injustices and group compensation of $50 million for a community trust foundation. Individual compensation was not included in their position.

While the US Commission report was stirring

10,046 Japanese Americans were interned in Manzanar, California. "You had the dust storm come through...You either get in bed and cover yourself with a sheet or just stand out there and suffer. You couldn't even see three feet in front of you, and then by the time the dust storm was *settled, you had at least a half inch of dust right on your sheet when you got under it." Tom Watanabe,* **And Justice for All** *(Random House, 1984), p. 95.*

Photo: Library of Congress 106998-LCA 351 3M-26.

The Japanese American Redress Movement

The seeds of the Japanese American redress struggle were planted much earlier than in Canada, in the early 1970s. By 1977-78, the Japanese American Citizens' League (JACL), the national organization for Japanese Americans, had established a Redress Committee which advocated redress in the form of individual compensation and a trust fund to promote the social, cultural, and educational interests of Japanese Americans.

In 1980, responding to pressure from the JACL, Congress established a Commission on Wartime Relocation and Internment of Civilians (CWRIC), concerning both Japanese Americans and Aleuts in Alaska. In 1981, the Commission conducted hearings, heard testimony, and examined relevant documents, to review their uprooting, and to recommend appropriate remedies.

In February 1983, the Commission concluded that the uprooting and internment of Japanese Americans was not a military necessity, and that Japanese Americans were the victims of injustices caused by "race prejudice, war hysteria, and a failure of political leadership" (*Personal Justice Denied*, p. 24). As redress they recommended

- an Acknowledgement of the injustices by Congress, signed by the President

- a fund for educational and humanitarian purposes

- individual compensation of $20,000 to survivors who were removed from the coast

Gordon Hirabayashi

In May 1942 Gordon Hirabayashi, a Quaker and a pacifist, refused to register and deliberately violated the curfew imposed on Japanese Americans. In a writtten statement at the time, the 24-year-old Hirabayashi justified his actions: "I consider it my duty to maintain the democratic standards for which this nation lives. Therefore, I must refuse this order for evacuation" (Quoted in *Justice at War* [Oxford University Press, 1983], p. 88). Forty-four years later, in February 1986, his conviction was reversed on the grounds that the government had concealed evidence supporting Hirabayashi's allegation that the internment was not a military necessity. His victory bolstered the redress campaign in both the US and Canada by confirming documentary evidence that the mass uprooting in both countries was a gross violation of civil rights.

Hirabayashi, who lives in Edmonton, is now Canadian and a well known member of the NAJC Council. His historical perspective and strong belief in individual rights helped shape the NAJC's redress principles.

Gordon Hirabayashi, NAJC Council member from Edmonton, at a council meeting in Vancouver, May 1987. Photo: Connie Kadota.

68

WARTIME CONVICTIONS OF THREE JAPANESE AMERICANS OVERTURNED

While the JACL continued lobbying to gain support for the Commission's recommendation in the House of Representatives and the Senate, in the courts a trio of coram nobis cases, or retrials, overturned the convictions of three American citizens who had defied the orders against Japanese Americans.

In 1942, four young Japanese Americans had instituted legal challenges: Gordon Hirabayashi and Minoru Yasui willfully broke the curfew order; Fred Korematsu chose to remain in the coast "prohibited area"; and Mitsuye Endo issued a writ of habeas corpus. Endo's case succeeded during the war, in December 1944, on the grounds that the US Constitution guarantees freedom of movement for all Americans. The US Supreme Court agreed that an American citizen could not be detained any longer than necessary to determine loyalty, which is why, in January 1945, before Japan's surrender, Japanese Americans began returning to the coast.

The other three Japanese Americans were convicted and had to wait some forty years before the courts found that the American government's curfew and uprooting policies were unjustified. The outcome vindicated all Japanese Americans, and fueled the political lobbying efforts of the JACL.

CLASS ACTION SUIT FAILS

In 1983, the National Council for Japanese American Redress, lead by William Hohri, brought a class action suit for damages on behalf of all Japanese Americans affected by the government actions. The case was plagued by procedural issues: which court should hear the appeals, and whether they could file a suit after forty years when the Statute of Limitations provides six years to sue the government.

The pursuit of a legal challenge also divided the Japanese American community. Resources were then split between funding the court case, and paying for the political lobbying necessary for the JACL's political campaign. On June 1, 1987, the US Supreme Court held that the case had been appealed to the wrong court, without addressing the substantive issue.

Former NAJC President, Gordon Kadota, organized an effective presentation on the up-rooting of Japanese Canadians to the Special Joint Committee on the Constitution, in November, 1980.
Photo: *Vancouver Sun.*

" *Our [Japanese Canadians'] history in Canada is a legacy of racism made legitimate by our political institutions, and we must somehow ensure that no group of Canadians will be subjected to the whims of political process as we were. We feel that this can only be done by entrenching a Charter of Rights in our constitution, unconditionally entrenching, beyond the reach of Parliament and beyond the reach of provincial legislatures.* "

Minutes of the Proceedings and Evidence of the Special Joint Committee of the Senate and of the House of Commons on the Constitution of Canada, *Wednesday, November 26, 1980.*

> *"It is immoral to turn our faces away from protecting the foundations of our great democracy so that no other group of men will ever take our laws lightly and make decisions on government action based on ancestry. Redress is morally right and just."*
>
> Grace Uyehara, Executive Director, Education Committee, Japanese American Citizens' League, quoted in Justice in Our Time (NAJC, 1988).

> *"My father was a veteran of the First World War and had fought with Canadians of Japanese descent in the Canadian army in the trenches in France and whose memorial, as you will know, is still there in Stanley Park commemorating the Japanese Canadians who died for Canada in the First World War. He spoke out against the internment, not because he was not a loyal Canadian; not because he was not prepared to fight in the war that we were engaged in, but because...what was being done to the sons and daughters of the comrades he fought with was contrary to the very British justice that we thought we were engaged in protecting in the fight against Nazism."*
>
> John Fraser, MP, Minutes of the Proceedings and Evidence of the Special Joint Committee of the Senate and of the House of Commons on the Constitution of Canada, Wednesday, November 26, 1980.

hope for a substantial settlement in Canada, Imai announced his committee's proposal to *Toronto Star* reporter Joe Serge ("Japanese Canadians Seek $50 Million for War Uprooting," February 14, 1983). His actions were untimely and premature, because at that very same time, NAJC President Gordon Kadota was just about to visit Japanese Canadian centres across Canada, to gather views on redress and to ask representatives to assist the NAJC to formulate a policy on this issue. This lack of co-ordination in the NAJC leadership would sow the seeds of dissension in the community.

In the summer of 1983, Imai seemed determined to force a community decision on redress by the fall. When news spread that the issue of redress might be resolved so quickly, without adequate community involvement, many Japanese Canadians who had long ago distanced themselves from community politics were drawn into the controversy. Almost overnight redress was no longer the cause of a few, but had become the focal point for a re-evaluation of past injustices by all.

Suddenly, process had become important. Consensus had become important. And Japanese Canadians had begun to realize that the question of individual versus group compensation needed a lot more work.

The beginnings of a truly national community movement surfaced at the NAJC conference convened by the National Redress Committee on the Labour Day weekend in September 1983. Dubbed a "Pre-Conference," the meeting was supposed to ratify the NRC's directive to seek group compensation, which in turn would lead to a National Conference celebrating that position. In a heated period of debate, both that position and the process of reaching it were challenged—and then rejected—by delegates from many Japanese

Canadian centres. Despite, or perhaps because of, the conflicts surrounding the NRC's loss of authority, the recognition emerged that a redress position should be set aside while the NAJC Council sought a more democratic means of representing the Japanese Canadians who were directly affected by the injustices of the 1940s.

The Labour Day conference had created a sense of urgency and crisis leading up to the next NAJC Council meeting—scheduled for Winnipeg in January 1984.

ART MIKI ELECTED PRESIDENT

The longstanding lack of co-ordinated action between the NAJC President and the NRC on the issue of redress had resulted in a leadership struggle, between the NAJC President in Vancouver and the Chair of the NRC in Toronto. It was this struggle that the members of the NAJC hoped to resolve at their Winnipeg meeting.

Art Miki had been active in the Japanese Canadian community since the 1977 centennial and had now become vocal on the redress issue. With his background in education, as a public school principal, as well as his extensive experience as a community leader in his hometown, Winnipeg, Miki was seen as the kind of leader who could bridge the divisions threatening to destroy the redress movement. Moreover, Winnipeg was a Japanese Canadian centre that geographically stood midway between the two large centres of community activities: Vancouver and Toronto.

Once Miki was elected President, he assumed the chair of the meeting. Almost immediately, three historic resolutions were passed that would remain the foundation of the redress movement until settlement on September 22, 1988, was finally achieved:

(top) **NAJC President Art Miki speaking at a community meeting on "Forms of Compensation," February 1985, Steveston, BC.** *Photo: Richmond Public Archives, Mark Patrick Collection.*

(above) **Hideichi Hamada, an issei, at the Steveston meeting; the photo was featured on the front page of the Richmond Review, February 27, 1985.** *Photo: Richmond Public Archives, Mark Patrick Collection.*

> " *RIGHT THE WRONG: The Parliament of Canada should officially acknowledge the mistreatment accorded to the Japanese in Canada during and after World War II and the Government of Canada should undertake negotiations to redress these wrongs.* "
>
> " *REVIEW THE WAR MEASURES ACT: Justice Canada should review the War Measures Act with a view to proposing the safeguards necessary to prevent a recurrence of the kind of mistreatment suffered by the Japanese in Canada during and after World War II.* "
>
> *Two recommendations on redress made in* Equality Now!, *p. 62, a report tabled in the House of Commons in March 1984 by the Special Committee on Participation of Visible Minorities in Canadian Society.*

1. The NAJC seeks acknowledgement from the Canadian Government of the injustices committed against Japanese Canadians during and after World War II.

2. Whereas the internment, exclusion and exiling of Japanese Canadians violated individual human rights and freedoms and destroyed the fabric of the community, the NAJC seeks redress in the form of monetary compensation.

3. Moreover, the NAJC seeks review and amendment of the War Measures Act and relevant sections of the Charter of Rights and Freedoms so that no Canadian will ever again be subjected to the wrongs committed against Japanese Canadians during World War II.

SPRING, 1984

As the redress campaign under President Art Miki's direction got underway, the government released, in March 1984, *Equality Now!,* a brief containing eighty recommendations to help visible minorities overcome the effects of racism and discrimination in Canada. The report was based on public hearings across the country during 1983, conducted by an all-party Special Committee on Participation of Visible Minorities in Canadian Society, chaired by Bob Daudlin, MP. Recommendation 33 in the report called for the government of Canada

- to issue an official acknowledgement of the injustices inflicted on Japanese Canadians
- to "undertake negotiations to redress these wrongs"
- to review the War Measures Act to prevent a recurrence of the injustices.

The three recommendations were similar, in principle, to the aims of the NAJC's resolutions at the January conference in Winnipeg.

For those Japanese Canadians who had been trying to raise public consciousness about redress, *Equality Now!* was a welcome endorsement of the cause. In response to this increased public consciousness, however, Prime Minister Pierre Trudeau hurled a massive insult at Japanese Canadians by flatly refusing to recognize the human rights value of redress. In a heated exchange with opposition leader Brian Mulroney, Trudeau stated:

> You're sick...if you're trying to take one wrong out of Canadian history and make great speeches about it and say that we're going to deal with this particular problem because there's a particular pressure group now.
>
> We could mount pressure groups across this country in many areas where there have been historic wrongs. I don't think it's the purpose of government to right the past...It cannot rewrite history. It is our purpose to be just in our time. (Canadian Press, Ottawa; cited in the Vancouver *Sun*, June 29, 1984)

Charging that Trudeau was blinded by narrow-mindedness, Mulroney promised that a Conservative government would recognize the significance of redress:

> I feel very strongly that Canadian citizens whose rights were abused and violated and trampled upon indeed should be compensated...If there was a Conservative government I can assure you we would be compensating Japanese Canadians. (*Globe and Mail*, May 16, 1984)

Compensate internees for unfair treatment, Mulroney urges PM

By RICHARD CLEROUX

Conservative Leader Brian Mulroney says he is in favor of compensation for Japanese Canadians who were unfairly interned during the Second World War.

Mr. Mulroney said in an interview yesterday that the Japanese Canadians "are not looking for overwhelming compensation.

"They're looking for symbolism and reassurance," he said. "I feel very strongly that Canadian citizens whose rights were abused and violated and trampled upon indeed should be compensated," he said.

Mr. Mulroney said he disagrees with Prime Minister Pierre Trudeau's stand that to compensate Japanese Canadians would mean the Government would have to compensate other groups.

"I don't swallow Mr. Trudeau's line about going back to the Acadians and Indians and all that nonsense," he said. "The fact of the matter is, it was 30 years ago and Canadian citizens were arbitrarily deprived of their rights and this should not happen. If there was a Conservative government I can assure you we would be compensating Japanese Canadians."

Mr. Mulroney did not say what he had in mind by way of compensation.

Mr. Mulroney and his wife Mila were in Toronto yesterday campaigning for the ethnic vote in a schedule that included four separate interviews at MTV, a multicultural television channel in the city, a reception for the ethnic press and a big evening reception in a north end hotel for about 1,000 party fund raisers from the various ethnic communities.

Mr. Mulroney repeated the commitment to fight for minority rights that he had made in Winnipeg March 29. He said there is no greater vocation for a politician in this country than to fight for the preservation of minority language and ethnic rights.

In Winnipeg he was booed and hissed and told to go back East when he made that commitment; in Toronto last night they applauded heartily. They even applauded when he spoke a few words of French, which was a marked contrast to the insults and catcalls he provoked when he spoke a few words of French in Winnipeg.

Mr. Mulroney poked fun at Liberal Leadership candidate John Turner's stand on the minority language rights issue.

"We've got that great pillar of consistency, Mr. Turner," Mr. Mulroney said sarcastically. "Now there's a guy who knows his mind . . . both of them.

"He began by opposing bilingualism in Manitoba, then he wound up supporting Bill 101 in uebec.

"It's hard to figure him out, except that I'm told that tomorrow he's going to announce that he's in favor of full and total bilingualism . . . in Rochester, Detroit and Gary, Ind."

Earlier in the day, Mr. Mulroney and his wife toured the Toronto Sun and met the publisher and the editorial board at The Globe and Mail.

"If there was a Conservative government I can assure you we would be compensating Japanese Canadians." **Globe and Mail, May 16, 1984.**

The Canadian Charter of Rights Does Not Protect Us

Canada is a signatory to the United Nations Convention on Human Rights which states that individuals must never be discriminated against on the basis of race, ethnic or national origin, even in a crisis. The Canadian Charter of Rights and Freedoms proclaims similar freedoms but they are subject to political will and not truly entrenched rights. Section 33 of the Charter allows Parliament and the provincial Legislatures to override these civil rights by simply declaring this intention in the legislation. In other words, by stating in the Act that the Charter of Rights does not apply, the government is not bound by the equality rights such as freedom from discrimination on the basis of racial ancestry.

Known as the "override clause," Section 33 has long been considered a serious loophole. An example of the way Section 33 can be used occurred when the Supreme Court of Canada struck down Quebec legislation requiring shop signs to be in French. In a controversial move, the Quebec legislature invoked Section 33 of the Charter to override the human rights section of the Charter that had invalidated the previous sign law.

Although the Emergencies Act which replaced the War Measures Act in 1988 does not contain an override provision, a future Parliament or possibly a cabinet acting as governor in council could amend the Emergencies Act to invoke Section 33, or could pass other legislation to legalize discrimination similar to that which caused the injustices suffered by Japanese Canadians. The only way to entrench the equality rights protections contained in the Charter of Rights and Freedoms is by amending the Charter so that no government can ever trample on the rights of individuals.

GOVERNMENT OFFERS REGRETS AND A $5 MILLION FOUNDATION

Trudeau's negative attitude towards the historical injustices suffered by Japanese Canadians no doubt governed the meagre gesture towards redress made by his Minister of State for Multiculturalism, David Collenette, in response to the *Equality Now!* brief.

Collenette stated that the Trudeau government would not issue an official "acknowledgement," arguing that the actions of the government in the 1940s, though unjust, were legal under the powers of the War Measures Act. They would merely make a general statement of "regret," along with a token $5 million grant for a proposed "Canadian Foundation for Racial Justice" to combat racism and to assist its victims—but nothing would be provided directly for Japanese Canadians, or even the Japanese Canadian community.

According to the NAJC, the government was evading the recommendations of the all-party committee responsible for *Equality Now!*—an "acknowledgement" tied to a "negotiated settlement." Worse still, the government dismissed the call for a review of the War Measures Act, and assured Canadians that the new Charter of Rights and Freedoms was adequate to protect them against the injustices inflicted on Japanese Canadians.

In actuality, the Charter enacted by the Trudeau government contains a major loophole: Section 33 allows the federal or provincial government to override the rights of individuals which are supposedly guaranteed by the Charter. Trudeau was correct in saying that the internment of Japanese Canadians under the War Measures Act would have been illegal had the Charter of Rights existed then. What he failed to add, however, is that any government could still invoke Section 33

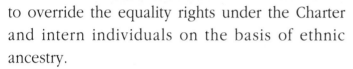

15-mile road camp.
*Photo: Japanese
Canadian Cultural
Centre, Toronto.*

to override the equality rights under the Charter and intern individuals on the basis of ethnic ancestry.

Trudeau's refusal to review the War Measures Act was not surprising. After all, his government had been the only government since World War II to invoke the War Measures Act and to apply it to a domestic crisis. In October and November of 1970, in response to two kidnappings by the Front de Libération du Québec, a state of "apprehended insurrection" was deemed to exist in Quebec and individual rights were violated. Trudeau had stridently defended his use of this extreme emergency legislation, so that a review could be seen as tacit acknowledgement that his own government's actions could be challenged as an abuse of rights.

Partly due to the widespread media coverage of the *Equality Now!* brief, the question of redress for Japanese Canadians was transformed into a national issue. Canadians became much more aware of the NAJC's struggle for justice. At the time, unfortunately, the NAJC Council found itself scrambling to formulate a plan of action, especially in light of the controversy stirred by the recommendations in the report. Lacking experience in planning strategy, they naively acquiesced to government pressure for a compensation figure. At an April meeting in

" *The principles of democracy were betrayed when the government, instead of invoking the full force of the law to protect Japanese Canadians against racist agitation, incarcerated the* **victims** *of race prejudice and, without consent, liquidated properties and belongings to compel the victims to pay for their own internment. The people of Canada were abused when they were unfairly led to believe that Japanese Canadians threatened the nation's security...*

" *In consequence of the abrogation of the rights and freedoms of Japanese Canadians during and after World War II, the National Association of Japanese Canadians calls on the Government of Canada to acknowledge its responsibility to compensate Japanese Canadians for injustices suffered and seeks a commitment from the Government of Canada to enter into negotiations towards a just and honourable settlement of this claim.* "

From "The Call for Redress," the final section of the NAJC's brief,
Democracy Betrayed, *submitted to the government on
November 21, 1984.*

A family in an internment house, Tashme, 1943.

Photo: Japanese Canadian Cultural Centre, Toronto.

Vancouver, the Council passed a motion for $500 million compensation. The proposed figure of $20,000 compensation per individual for Japanese Americans had provided the guideline.

Such a large figure, without an objective basis in actual losses, had potentially disastrous political consequences. The redress issue could have died in the squabble over money, and the Japanese Canadian community could have lost the opportunity of undertaking a meaningful process of dialogue to resolve the past injustices, based on the actual Canadian context and circumstances. For these reasons, the dollar figure was set aside when the redress brief was prepared, and never made public. Instead, the NAJC Council chose to seek a negotiated settlement, arguing the case for redress on the basis of the historical and documentary evidence. At that time, the public's understanding of the injustices which had been committed was just beginning to emerge, and large monetary demands might have alienated Canadians at this early stage—a situation which the government would certainly have used to undermine the NAJC's redress campaign.

NAJC REJECTS COLLENETTE'S OFFER

While President Art Miki publicly rejected Collenette's offer as an inadequate form of redress, the NAJC's National Redress

Committee precipitated a serious division within the NAJC. Early in June, some council members reported to Miki that various elderly Japanese Canadians were secretly being invited to Ottawa by George Imai, still chair of the National Redress Committee, to a special ceremony at which the government would issue an official statement of "regret." Miki called an emergency telephone conference to prevent the National Redress Committee from undermining its own organization's opposition to the government. Faced with the threat of disunity, the NAJC Council

Sutekichi (George) and Itoh Miyagawa, an issei couple, are among the audience of over 500 people who attended "Redress for Japanese Canadians."
Photo: Ian Lindsay, Vancouver Sun.

moved to dissolve the National Redress Committee, and Miki became the official NAJC spokesperson on all redress matters.

Disgruntled with this decision, George Imai subsequently joined forces with his Toronto ally, NAJC Vice-President Jack Oki, to begin a campaign to challenge the NAJC as the genuinely representative organization for Japanese Canadians. Working primarily in the Toronto area, they enlisted the support of the Toronto Japanese Canadian Citizens' Association (TJCCA), and by the fall of 1985 had formed their own Japanese

Community forum, "Redress for Japanese Canadians," at the Japanese Language School, Vancouver, August 1984. From left to right: Tatsuo Kage, Japanese language interpreter, David Suzuki, Tom Shoyama, Roy Miki, Ann Sunahara. Joy Kogawa was unable to attend, but Irene Nemeth, seated behind Suzuki, delivered her speech.
Photo: Ian Lindsay, Vancouver Sun.

77

Cover of Democracy Betrayed *(NAJC, 1984).*

DEMOCRACY BETRAYED
THE CASE FOR REDRESS

Public Archives of Canada

A submission to the Government of Canada on the violation of rights and freedoms of Japanese Canadians during and after World War II

NATIONAL ASSOCIATION OF JAPANESE CANADIANS

At the release of the NAJC brief, Democracy Betrayed, *in Vancouver, BC, on November 21, 1984. From left to right: Archie Miyashita, Saul Kadonaga, and Motoi Iwanaka. Kadonaga and Iwanaka, both deceased, were issei members of the Vancouver JCCA Redress Committee. Photo: Ralph Bower, Vancouver Sun.*

Canadian National Redress Association of Survivors (or the "Survivors' Group" as it came to be called).

As the controversy with Collenette subsided, John Turner succeeded Trudeau as leader of the Liberal party and called an election for September 1984. Turner did not endorse Trudeau's inflexible position and promised the NAJC he would keep the redress issue open.

With renewed hope offered by the Conservatives and Liberals, and the already committed support of the NDP, the NAJC awaited the election results with some prospect that a new government could be willing to work towards a negotiated settlement.

NAJC SUBMITS A REDRESS BRIEF TO THE GOVERNMENT

When the Progressive Conservatives won a sweeping victory in the fall election of 1984, Art Miki wrote immediately to

Prime Minister Brian Mulroney, congratulating him on his victory, and requesting a meeting to discuss redress.

Soon thereafter, on November 21, 1984, Miki submitted the NAJC's brief to the government. *Democracy Betrayed: The Case for Redress* called on the government to acknowledge the injustices suffered by Japanese Canadians during and after

World War II, to enter into negotiations to compensate them, and to entrench equality rights in the Charter of Rights and Freedoms.

JACK MURTA THREATENS UNILATERAL DECISION

The following day, to the great disappointment of the NAJC, Jack Murta, the Minister of State for Multiculturalism, was quoted in the *Globe and Mail* as saying: "The older Japanese Canadians, the ones who were actually involved in the uprooting for the most part don't want compensation" (*Globe and Mail*, November 22, 1984).

This theme would be played out for a number of years by the government in their attempt to discredit the NAJC as the legitimate voice of Japanese Canadians.

Five days later, when Murta met with NAJC representatives, he warned them that he intended to settle the redress issue quickly, perhaps before Christmas. The NAJC countered his threat of unilateral action by organizing its first full-scale letter campaign to stop him. The protest was successful—it led to a formal meeting between the NAJC and three government officials representing Murta.

Vancouver Sun, *June 22, 1984. Cartoon by Roy Peterson.*

" *We're a very small group in numbers. And so the policy of dispersing Japanese Canadians across this country, even after the defeat of Japan, worked beyond the wildest dreams of politicians. And forty years later, most of the people of my generation are still hiding in the woodwork and not wanting to speak. As Aunt Emily says in* Obasan, *our tongues were cut off. It takes a while for the nerves to grow back.* "

Joy Kogawa, in conversation with Robert Fulford, The Case for Redress: Information (*NAJC, 1984*).

" *It is as an act of citizenship and because we refuse to see democracy betrayed that we seek an honourable resolution to the injustices of the war years. In calling for redress, we affirm our pride in our country and our faith in the principles which determine this nation as a democracy.* "

From the Introduction to Democracy Betrayed *(NAJC, 1984).*

Mennonite Central Committee Supports Japanese Canadians

In October 1984, the Mennonite Central Committee Canada issued an official apology to Canadians of Japanese ancestry who were unjustly uprooted, interned and dispossessed during World War II. The organization acknowledged that although it was not responsible for the injustices, some Mennonites had benefitted by being able to buy confiscated property, especially farms in the lower Fraser Valley. At the January meeting of the Central Committee in Leamington, Ontario, a motion was passed to contribute a minimum of $10,000 towards a scholarship fund to commemorate Japanese Canadian internment.

NEGOTIATIONS PROMISED

It was on December 15, 1984, in Winnipeg, that the NAJC Council met with government representatives Doug Bowie, Orest Kruhlak, and Anne Scotton, for a long and candid discussion of the redress issue. An agreement was struck to undertake a process of negotiation on the wording of the official acknowledgement, the amount of compensation, and the steps needed to prevent a recurrence of such injustices. There was to be a flexible time frame to ensure a meaningful process. A press release issued by Murta announced the agreement.

The NAJC prepared for negotiations by establishing a Negotiation Team.

That night, amid the excitement that a settlement finally appeared in sight, the redress issue hit the national news, and there on the CBC broadcast was a Japanese flag behind barbed wire. It was clear that the NAJC still had a long way to go in making the media and Canadians aware that the violation of rights was carried out against Canadians who happened to be of Japanese ancestry, and not against Japanese nationals who had happened to find themselves in Canada. This error foreshadowed the major setback the community would experience with the government the following month, when the NAJC believed serious negotiations were to begin.

NAJC Council posing with government officials after agreement to begin negotiations. Talks soon broke down when Jack Murta reneged on the agreement. Seated with Art Miki, left to right: Orest Kruhlak, Anne Scotton, and Doug Bowie.
Courtesy of Art Miki.

Harold Hirose

Throughout the redress campaign, Harold Hirose was NAJC Treasurer. In public meetings he often spoke of his experience, as a veteran of the Second World War, concerning his property near the Patullo Bridge in Surrey:

"I had a five acre property of land in Surrey. It was partly cleared. And this land was taken away from me. I registered to the

Custodian of Enemy Property, with the understanding that they would return it to me when I came back to BC after the war. But without my consent, as you all know, they confiscated this land and they sold it for the measly sum of $36. After taking the registration fees and legal fees, I received a cheque of $15. When I was being discharged, the judge advocate's office in Winnipeg felt that this was an outrageous thing, and they wrote a letter to the Minister at the

time, Ian Mackenzie, and so on and so forth, but I was refused my land. The irony of the whole thing is that the people who took over the land, our land, the Fraser Valley lands, were the Veterans' Land Act people who were supposed to be looking after the veterans like myself coming back. So I applied for the return of my own land, and after much correspondence, I was told that I had to go through the same route as any other soldier, that I had to go on that homestead route" (*Spirit of Redress* [JC Publications, 1989], pp. 35-36).

Uprooted and sent to a sugar beet farm in Manitoba, Harold helped spearhead an organization for Japanese Canadians in Manitoba. Because such an organization was ruled illegal by the BC Security Commission, they met secretly, often in Chinese hotels:

"The weather in the prairies in 1942, that year was one of the most severe winters, and the temperature was down almost 50 below zero. With this severe winter coming, and after harvesting was over, well we all had to be cooped up in this shack, and this was where the majority of the Japanese people felt that we had to do something. That was the start of the organization of the Manitoba Japanese Joint Council, which became the nucleus of the

Manitoba JCCA" (*Spirit of Redress* [JC Publications, 1989], p. 131).

When nisei were allowed into the Canadian Armed Forces in 1945, Harold joined up and served in Burma and India. Later, in 1947, as the representative of the Manitoba JCCA, he became a founding member of the National JCCA, which became the NAJC in 1980.

(above) **Harold Hirose at the Ottawa Redress Rally, April 1988.** *Photo: Gordon King.*

(left) **Harold Hirose in Poona, India, August 1945.** Courtesy of Harold Hirose.

MULTICULTURALISM

— news release —

M-12/84-24

THE FOLLOWING IS THE TEXT OF A JOINT NEWS RELEASE
ISSUED BY THE MINISTER OF STATE FOR MULTICULTURALISM AND
THE NATIONAL ASSOCIATION OF JAPANESE CANADIANS

WINNIPEG, December 15, 1984 - At the request of the Minister of
State for Multiculturalism, the Honourable Jack Murta, senior officials of
the federal government met today with council members from across Canada of
the National Association of Japanese Canadians to design a consultation
process to allow federal government officials to recommend a course of
action on redress for Japanese Canadians.

A full and frank discussion was undertaken establishing a
negotiation process between the NAJC and the federal government.

Discussion has started on:

1) the timeframe for the process of negotiation
2) the wording and content of the official acknowledgement of the
   injustices suffered by Japanese Canadians
3) the amount and nature of compensation
4) the steps that should be taken to prevent the re-occurrence of
   such injustices
5) the possibilities of a series of meetings with Japanese Canadian
   communities across the country

- 30 -

Information: Allan Higdon (819) 997-9900

Canadä

Press release issued by Jack Murta, December 15, 1984, announcing a negotiation process.

82

NOT NEGOTIATION, ONLY CONSULTATION

A chronology published in the first issue of the *NAJC Newsletter* (March 1985) records the series of events in January 1985 that led to the rapid disintegration of talks with Jack Murta:

January 4:

At the first negotiation session with Orest Kruhlak and Anne Scotton, the NAJC presented a proposal for the negotiation process, and discussions began on various redress matters, such as the wording of the acknowledgement, citizenship for Japanese Canadians expelled from Canada, pardons for those convicted under the War Measures Act, and steps to ensure that these injustices will never be inflicted on other Canadians.

At this first negotiation meeting, the Government stated that it wanted to reach a settlement by January 29. The NAJC was shocked to hear that this deadline was a political decision and that non-compliance by the NAJC with this date could lead the Government to either unilaterally put forth its own redress package, or to shelve the issue for good.

The NAJC Negotiation Team rejected the imposition of an arbitrary deadline for negotiations.

January 12:

At the second negotiation session, the NAJC was informed that the deadline of January 29 had been extended until February 20, the final date by which all substantive redress matters had to be resolved. The Government also now said it did not consider the meetings negotiation sessions, but simply "consultations."

January 18:
Representatives of the NAJC met with Mr. Murta in Vancouver and learned that he was firm in his new position of January 12 that he did not intend to negotiate with the NAJC. He said the Government was willing to offer an Acknowledgement and a $6 million educational trust fund. He did not present the Government's offer in writing, but admitted that the fund would not be controlled by the Japanese Canadian community.

The NAJC reiterated its position that a meaningful resolution to redress had to be the product of direct and full negotiations with the NAJC and its community. Mr. Murta agreed to try to facilitate a meeting with Prime Minister Brian Mulroney to discuss the NAJC's concerns.

January 24:
The NAJC Council held a telephone conference on the Government's approach to a redress settlement, and by vote, agreed both to reject any unilateral action and to press for the continuation of the negotiation process.

January 28:
The NAJC called a press conference in Ottawa to inform the Canadian public of its objection to the Government's intention of moving unilaterally with an arbitrarily imposed deadline. The NAJC stated that a meaningful settlement had to be the product of direct and substantial negotiations with the NAJC.

January 28-29:
The NAJC met with the two opposition

"*For 40 years the Government of Canada has shown little interest in righting the wrongs committed on our people during and after World War II. Although we applaud the announced intentions of the present federal administration in wanting to negotiate a settlement with us, we deplore the pressure that suddenly within 60 days we must come to an agreement on the many complex questions surrounding a prospective settlement.*"

From a letter from Art Miki to Jack Murta, January 18, 1985.

Kumaye Miyai at the Steveston docks, just prior to the uprooting, 1942. Photo: Japanese Canadian Cultural Centre, Toronto.

> " *You, who deal in lifeless figures, files, and statistics could never measure the depth of hurt and outrage dealt out to those of us who love this land. It is because we **are** Canadians, that we protest the violation of our birthright.* "
>
> Muriel Kitagawa, from a letter to the Custodian of Enemy Property, July 8, 1943, This Is My Own *(Talonbooks, 1985), pp. 184-5.*

(right) **Art Miki and NAJC Strategy Committee meeting with John Turner in Ottawa, January 1985.** *Photo: Wes Fujiwara.*

(below right): **NAJC Strategy Committee meeting with Ed Broadbent in Ottawa, January 1985. Seated in the background are observers Mrs. T. Umezuki, from Toronto, and Amy Yamazaki, from Ottawa.** *Photo: Wes Fujiwara.*

Art Miki at the NAJC press conference in Ottawa, January 1985. Seated with Miki are Mrs. T. Umezuki, Roger Obata, and National Press Gallery staff person. *Photo: Wes Fujiwara.*

party leaders, John Turner of the Liberals and Ed Broadbent of the NDP, to explain the NAJC's position. Both Turner and Broadbent assured the NAJC that their parties would not support an all-party resolution proposed by Jack Murta without the consent of the NAJC. They also agreed to urge the Conservative government to continue the negotiation process with the NAJC.

January 31:
Unable to attain all-party support for the Government's redress package, Jack Murta announced that he was suspending action for the time being.

ACTION ON REDRESS IS SUSPENDED

Jack Murta's offer of a $6 million educational trust fund was essentially the same as David Collenette's offer from the Liberal government—an offer that Prime Minister Brian

Mulroney had criticized as inadequate. Having ruled out "negotiation," Murta also rejected "compensation," using instead his own word, "memorialization," to define the function of the trust fund. The optimism generated by the press release of December 15 had evaporated in one short month.

The NAJC had been initiated quickly into the complexity of the political process. Though the dead end reached with Murta had been a major disappointment, the alliances struck with the Liberals and the NDP, as well as the detailed media coverage of conflicting views on the term "negotiation," were learning experiences.

The NAJC had succeeded in stopping a unilateral settlement by the government, and shown by its determination that the process of achieving a just and honourable settlement was as important as the outcome.

NAJC UNDERTAKES ECONOMIC LOSSES STUDY

With no prospects for further negotiations, and with Murta threatening to close the door completely on redress, the NAJC was soon under some pressure to acquiesce. Some believed that if the NAJC did not accept Murta's offer, Japanese Canadians would receive nothing. Some wanted the NAJC to accept an acknowledgement and the memorial fund, and then press further for a compensation package. Some outside observers urged acceptance by arguing that public interest in redress had already peaked two months before, in December 1984.

At this critical juncture in the campaign, the NAJC Council met in Calgary on February 2-3, 1985, to assess Murta's position on redress. One key decision established the overall direction of the movement in the years ahead. To maintain a stronger and, in the long run, more secure

NAJC Council Meeting, Calgary, February 2-3, 1985

Disappointed that Jack Murta had reneged on his commitment to negotiate with the NAJC, as announced in the December 15, 1984, press release, the NAJC wrote to Prime Minister Mulroney with three requests:

"1. that a redress settlement must be acceptable to the NAJC and our community and would include as one package the wording and content of the Acknowledgement, monetary and non-monetary compensation;

"2. that the government will discuss with the NAJC amendments to the War Measures Act and the Charter of Rights and Freedoms to ensure that Canadians are protected from the injustices suffered by Japanese Canadians; and

"3. that discussions on compensation be deferred until the feasibility of a socio-economic study of the wartime treatment of Japanese Canadians is assessed, as was agreed to by the government's representatives."

When Murta refused to co-operate in the socio-economic study, the NAJC went ahead and retained Price Waterhouse to do their own socio-economic study.

On May 15, 1985, NAJC representatives met with Murta in Winnipeg to relay the NAJC position that the acknowledge-ment and compensation must be kept together as one package.

NAJC Council meeting in Calgary, February 2-3, 1985.

Photo: Tamio Wakayama.

The Japanese Canadian National Redress Association of Survivors

A petition published in the *Canada Times* on March 22, 1985, announced the formation of the Japanese Canadian National Redress Association of Survivors (JCNRAS). It was initiated by a handful of Japanese Canadians who opposed the NAJC's strong position in favour of individual compensation. They favoured an acknowledgement of the injustices and group compensation in the form of a "memorial trust fund or foundation."

In actuality, JCNRAS reflected the views of George Imai, former chair of the NAJC National Redress Committee, who was a vocal opponent of individual compensation—and became the most vocal critic of the NAJC after his committee was dissolved in June 1984.

Some prominent issei were listed as members of JCNRAS, and for a time their names alone threatened to create divisions in the community. The NAJC was labelled a "radical" organization, whereas JCNRAS claimed to speak for the "silent majority." Perhaps the most damaging aspect of their campaign to undermine the NAJC was their claim that the issei suffered and lost the most. The tactic drew on a cultural tradition of honouring one's elders, but in the context of the political struggle, it stirred conflicts between the generations and many issei were subject to pressures that were unwarranted.

As the redress campaign wore on, JCNRAS representatives continued to attack the NAJC, but did not hold community meetings or sponsor other redress activities.

> *"[George Imai] has been promoting these divisions in the name of the issei, who really long for unity. When he pits them against the rest of the community this is the most hurtful thing possible."*
>
> *Joy Kogawa, from "Sabotage Claimed in Handling Redress," by Nancy Knickerbocker, Vancouver Sun, May 31, 1986.*

"bargaining" position, the NAJC resolved to seek a single-package redress settlement. The Council rejected the strategy of accepting an acknowledgement first, then negotiating for compensation, believing that the issue would most likely languish, and then die. The government would no doubt argue that they—and therefore the Canadian public—had formally exonerated Japanese Canadians, thereby distancing themselves from the further issue of compensation. By seeking one package, the NAJC would not have to negotiate piece-meal. Redress would be resolved once and for all—or it would be left unresolved if the government chose not to negotiate a just and honourable settlement with the NAJC. It was a difficult decision to make, because the Council was very aware that seniors were passing away without the satisfaction of hearing the acknowledgement. On the other hand, given the aging population of the wartime Japanese

Canadians, the opportunity of a meaningful settlement would likely not come again in their lifetime, once an acknowledgement had been given.

MURTA ATTEMPTS TO USE SPLINTER JAPANESE CANADIAN GROUP

On June 20, 1985, in the dying days of his work with the NAJC, Murta wrote in a letter to Art Miki that the "Survivors' Group," the splinter organization working in opposition to the NAJC, "be invited to participate in any future discussions we may have." Earlier, on June 4, this group, represented by Jack Oki and George Imai, had held a press conference in Ottawa where they claimed to speak on behalf of the "silent majority" of Japanese Canadians who did not support the NAJC's redress position. The Minister had perhaps hoped to use the "Survivors' Group" to coerce the NAJC into compromising its demand for a negotiated settlement, which the government knew would include the issue of individual compensation.

According to spokesperson Imai, the position of the "Survivors' Group" was very similar to the government's offer. In a Vancouver *Sun* article on his Ottawa press conference, he was quoted as saying, "We're on the same wavelength," referring to the government's offer of an "apology" and a memorial foundation (Vancouver *Sun,* June 5, 1985).

THE PRICE WATERHOUSE STUDY BEGINS

While engaged in these heated confrontations with Murta, the NAJC made a major decision that would eventually affect the outcome of the redress movement. On May 16, 1985, an announcement was made that Price Waterhouse had agreed to

(above) **Taishodo store in the prewar Japanese Canadian community—one of the businesses confiscated by the Custodian.**
Photo: Vancouver Public Library #11804.

(top) **Confiscated cars at Hastings Park, 1942.** *Photo: Vancouver Public Library #1374.*

"*The Charter does not ensure that it will not happen again. A nation that confines itself to high-faluting talk, but does not sit down and negotiate to provide compensation to the people whom it interned 40 years ago, is not likely to remember the episode for long. If, however, we demonstrate that our concern is tangible by compensating the survivors, we are demonstrating that we believe it should never have happened, and we make it less likely that it will ever happen again. This is the best we can do, at the same time it is the least that we can do.*"

Thomas Berger, Reflections on Redress
(Greater Vancouver JCCA Redress Committee, 1986).

Art Miki at a meeting in Ottawa with Otto Jelinek, January 1986. *Photo: Bryce Kanbara.*

undertake a socio-economic study of losses suffered by Japanese Canadians as a result of the mass uprooting in the 1940s. The NAJC had needed an incentive to mobilize their community's participation in public meetings and fundraising events. The Price Waterhouse project, which required financial backing from Japanese Canadians, could provide a dynamic focal point.

Paradoxically, Murta's refusal to negotiate had created the impetus for grassroots political empowerment in the local Japanese Canadian communities across the country. The redress movement had penetrated the deepest layers of their awareness and now, finally, the issue came to dominate the lives of many Japanese Canadians. As various petitions circulated in support of the NAJC, and as letter-writing campaigns were mounted, a series of house-meetings were organized where individuals could receive redress news and share stories of their internment experiences. This community awakening contributed directly to the growing strength of the NAJC—not in spite of, but because of Murta's failure to resolve the redress issue.

OTTO JELINEK REPLACES MURTA

Discussions with Murta ended when Otto Jelinek, Minister of Sports, was given the additional responsibility for Multiculturalism in August 1985. The NAJC hoped a new Minister might bring a more sympathetic—and meaningful—approach to the redress issue, but Jelinek not only adopted Murta's position, he also assumed a much more overtly aggressive stance. The facade of conciliatory concern displayed by Murta was replaced by a hardline approach. The "will of the majority" of Canadians, so Jelinek argued, was against financial redress, so he would not use taxpayers' money to compensate Japanese Canadians.

Jelinek quickly ruled out "negotiations," and played the role of a tough-minded politician by threatening the NAJC with his "take it or leave it" offer—Murta's offer with perhaps another $2 to $4 million added to the memorial foundation. Most importantly, though, he stirred up controversy by refusing to recognize the NAJC as the official Japanese Canadian representative organization.

Murta had alleged that elderly Japanese Canadians were opposed to compensation, implying that the NAJC did not represent the Japanese Canadians who had been interned. His successor, Otto Jelinek, pushed this view to an extremity by rejecting the NAJC's right to speak on behalf of Japanese Canadians at all.

JELINEK ALSO MOVES TOWARDS UNILATERAL ACTION

By late November, after dodging the issue for months, Jelinek tried to stir dissension in the community by accusing the NAJC of extremism, saying that the organization was run by young radicals. With a strange twist of logic, he also publicly declared that he would not "insult"

During 1985-86, while the NAJC struggled with Otto Jelinek, much educational work was undertaken to impress upon Canadians the value of redress as a human rights issue. Here a group of volunteers in Toronto are mailing out the NAJC Newsletter, *January 1987. From left to right: Wes Fujiwara, Jennifer Hashimoto, Joy Kogawa, Charlotte Chiba, Mary Obata, Misao Fujiwara, Roger Obata. Photo: Ben Fiber.*

> "*We must remember that Canadian citizens whose rights were abrogated because of their racial ancestry were forced to suffer social, economic, and personal losses on a scale unprecedented in the recent history of our country. Surely, an honourable and meaningful settlement of the wrongs resulting from unjust Government actions must be determined through a process of negotiations with those who were wronged.*"

From a press release issued by the NAJC, January 28, 1986, after a meeting with Otto Jelinek in Ottawa.

The Canadian Multicultural Council

In November 1985, the Canadian Multicultural Council (CMC), a government-appointed advisory group for Otto Jelinek, passed a motion attacking the NAJC's redress program. In a press release, issued without discussions with the NAJC, they essentially backed the government with a package of symbolic monetary awards, a multicultural foundation, and pension supplements based on age, health and economic need, not for injustices suffered.

Since the CMC was composed of individuals from various ethnic backgrounds, their motion left the impression—an intentional strategy—that many ethnic groups sided with the government against the NAJC's demands.

In February 1986, the CMC escalated their attack in a letter to the *Globe and Mail* in which they alleged the NAJC did not represent the victims of the injustices, and also argued against individual compensation.

By interfering in the negotiation process between Otto Jelinek and the NAJC, the CMC acted in such a partisan manner that their position itself became untenable. For instance, Navin M. Parekh, President of the Canadian Ethnocultural Council, chastized the CMC for attempting to influence the course of negotiations:

"The Canadian Ethnocultural Council represents [over 35] nationally constituted ethnic organizations, and the National Association of Japanese Canadians represents the Japanese community on our council. We feel strongly that no acceptable settlement of the redress issue can take place without ongoing negotiation with the NAJC. Although there are bound to be differences of opinion between the CMC and ethnic organizations from time to time, it undermines the council's credibility and damages the ethnic community as a whole for an organization such as the NAJC to be subjected to public attack" (From a letter to the editor, *Globe and Mail*, March 20, 1986).

Japanese Canadians by offering compensation. Then, having ruled out "negotiations" and "compensation," he adopted the strategy of soliciting advice from "Canadians at large" for an appropriate settlement, including Japanese Canadian individuals of his own choosing. Finally, like Murta one year before, he threatened to resolve the issue unilaterally.

But by this time, the Price Waterhouse study was well under way, and Japanese Canadians were much more unified in their support for the NAJC. Jelinek's attacks only strengthened their resolve to press more vigorously for negotiations. The NAJC Negotiation Team had met with him only once, on October 21, 1985, when nothing of substance had been discussed.

In response to Jelinek's threat of unilateral action, the NAJC again travelled to Ottawa in protest. On January 27, 1986, in one more effort to begin meaningful discussions, the Negotiation Team met with the Minister at his Multiculturalism offices in Hull, Quebec. He again refused to recognize the NAJC as the representative organization for the Japanese Canadian community, saying that other groups such as the "Survivors' Group" would be approached. He maintained that the "real survivors" had told him that they did not want compensation, accused the NAJC of dragging its feet, and threatened to act on the proposals of other groups. The NAJC, in turn, requested that the government not act until the Price Waterhouse report on economic losses was completed.

GOVERNMENT-APPOINTED MULTICULTURAL COUNCIL BACKS JELINEK

Perhaps frustrated by the NAJC's resistance to his tactics, Jelinek launched an indirect attack, focusing primarily on the NAJC's demand for a "negotiated" settlement which included direct compensation to the individual Japanese Canadians affected by the wartime injustices.

Jelinek's own government-appointed Canadian Multicultural Council, in a blatant demonstration of political bias, came out in defense of his offer by formulating "their own position" against the NAJC's call for compensation. At a time when newspaper editorials across the country, as well as many ethnic organizations and civil rights advocates, were urging the Prime Minister to honour his pre-election commitment to compensate Japanese Canadians, this tactic was so ill-timed and transparent, that it backfired.

With public sympathy for the NAJC on the rise, Jelinek's effort to undermine its credibility was soon perceived as both insensitive and hypo-critical. Ironically, the more aggressive he became, the more support the NAJC received from the media and the Canadian public. It was at this time that many ethnic and civil rights groups, including the Canadian Ethnocultural Council, representing over thirty-five national ethnic organizations, became much more vocal in their demand that the government negotiate a just and honourable settlement with the NAJC.

THE NAJC FORMULATES A POSITION

The Jelinek phase of the redress movement was tumultuous and frustrating. His attack on the NAJC created emotional upheaval in the community, and his overtures to the "Survivors' Group," for a time, appeared to disrupt the NAJC's campaign. This test of adversity, on the other hand, did have its advantanges. As the NAJC seemed beleaguered by political foes, outside the community with Jelinek, and inside the community with the "Survivors' Group," more and more grass-

NAJC Questionnaire on Forms of Compensation

In April 1986, the NAJC conducted a survey of Japanese Canadians across Canada to determine their views on redress. The results showed strong support for compensation as an element in a redress settlement. More of those who were directly affected by the injustices between 1942 and 1949 favoured individual compensation over community compensation or combined individual and community compensation.

The questionnaire effectively answered government charges that Japanese Canadians did not support individual compensation, and provided the NAJC with invaluable information to determine a grassroots position on redress.

Note: percentages do not total 100% because numbers have been rounded, and some respondents had no opinion.

FORMS OF COMPENSATION FAVOURED BY RESPONDENTS

	Individual	Community	Individual & Community	Individual Amount $
Vancouver	46%	18%	30%	27,000
Kamloops	38	25	28	30,000
Winnipeg	30	32	31	25,000
Hamilton	54	8	27	29,000
Toronto	41	25	23	31,000
Montreal	43	25	21	35,000

Price Waterhouse Study

Early in the redress campaign, the NAJC recognized the need for an estimate of economic losses resulting from the uprooting and dispossession of Japanese Canadians during and after World War II, to justify the demand for meaningful financial compensation. The NAJC, while in discussions with Jack Murta, explored the question of a joint study which could be used to educate Canadians on the enormity of material losses to Japanese Canadians, but as well create some parameters for negotiations. When talks broke down with Murta, the government flatly refused to be involved in the study.

At the time, in the spring of 1985, the NAJC had virtually no money to undertake such a substantial research project, but through personal connections an informal meeting was held with Phil Barter, partner in charge at the Vancouver Price Waterhouse office. Barter was sympathetic to the redress movement and

recalled the painful memory of watching some of his Japanese Canadian friends shipped away.

Price Waterhouse agreed to do the economic losses study under a contingent fee agreement, at a minimal cost of only $27,000. Their fees would be paid only if the NAJC achieved a redress settlement with the government.

The Price Waterhouse report, *Economic Losses of Japanese Canadians After 1941*, was released on May 8, 1986, and provided the first documented calculation of losses suffered by Japanese Canadians from 1941

The Bird Commission

The Royal Commission headed by Justice Henry Bird, which was established in 1947 to evaluate property losses by Japanese Canadians, was a gesture of political expediency, not a form of redress. Bird was allowed to consider only those losses resulting from the Custodian's sale at below market value—and the owners themselves had to prove market value. Bird had no jurisdiction to investigate other losses, and he could not question the "justice" of the government's policies. In the end, a mere $1.2 million ($11,040,000 in 1986 dollars) was given to those who applied.

LOSSES BEYOND THE SCOPE OF THE STUDY

There were no figures for "pain and suffering"—the humiliation of being branded "enemy alien," the emotional trauma of the uprooting, the breakup of families, and the harsh living conditions. Nor did it include a monetary figure for the violation of rights, wrongful internment, unjust liquidation of properties, destruction of the community, expulsion from Canada, and the shameful government policy requiring Japanese Canadians to pay for their internment.

Japanese Canadians who were being sent to Japan, at the train station, Slocan, BC, 1946. Photo: National Archives of Canada C47398.

to 1949. The research was based on documents in the National Archives, from files on individual Japanese Canadians kept by the Custodian of Enemy Property, the authority responsible for liquidating properties, houses, businesses, and personal belongings.

While the report deals with properties and businesses, it does not calculate possible economic growth had Japanese Canadians not been so completely dispossessed. For instance, in the area of logging, the study states: "Had Japanese Canadians continued to operate significant lumber companies ...they may well have participated significantly in the growth of the BC forest industry" (p. 58).

Ironically, it was the very resourcefulness of Japanese Canadians themselves, particularly after the war, that reduced their losses. Had they not assumed responsibility for their economic welfare, their losses would have been much higher. The government files, according to the Price Waterhouse researchers, "contain numerous references to the industry and drive of the Japanese Canadians from 1942 onwards. These qualities tended to mitigate the loss suffered by the community by reducing the period of loss. In addition, they suggest this community would have continued to improve its economic position if dispersal had not happened" (p. 27).

SUMMARY OF LOSSES IN 1986 DOLLARS

The Japanese Canadian community suffered a total economic loss of not less than $443 million, calculated in 1986 dollars.

Total income loss was

Income loss	$333,040,000
Fraser Valley farmland	49,314,000
Other real property	40,986,000
Fishing assets	10,350,000
Businesses	7,627,000
Other property	10,341,000
Education: Fees paid	1,380,000
Other losses	1,141,000
Less: Awards made by Bird Commission	11,040,000
TOTAL ECONOMIC LOSSES:	$443,139,000

Education for the Children

The Price Waterhouse study showed that Japanese Canadians often mitigated their losses through their own initiatives. Nowhere was this more evident than with the problem of education. When the federal government failed to provide schooling, as they had promised for those in the BC interior detention camps, Japanese Canadians themselves assumed responsibility for their childrens' education. Despite deficiencies in English language skills, the students scored high on the Stanford Achievement Tests administered in 1943-44-45. However, many children lost a year because of the disruption of their community. Some Japanese Canadians outside the BC camps, especially those sent to sugar beet farms in Alberta, were actually required to pay for the high school education of their children.

calculated at $333 million. Property loss, which includes Fraser Valley farms, houses, fishing boats, businesses, and other personal belongings, was estimated at $110 million.

Japanese Canadians in a communal kitchen at the internment camp in Slocan, BC. Photo: University of British Columbia, Special Collections.

George Honda Kakuno (1898 - 1990), an issei, was a dedicated supporter of redress and active on the NAJC Council as a representative of the Japanese Canadian community in Kelowna, BC. Here, at the NAJC Conference in Vancouver in May 1987, he reminded Japanese Canadians that a redress settlement must consider the needs of the smaller communities: "Even though we might build a fabulous facility in Vancouver, people in Kelowna or Vernon would not move. Please remember that those who stay in such towns may well be your father or mother" (Spirit of Redress [JC Publications, 1989], p. 90). *Photo: Connie Kadota.*

Polls Support Redress for Japanese Canadians

Throughout the campaign, the NAJC knew that public opinion would largely determine the government's position on redress. In March 1986, a national poll showed that 63% of Canadians supported redress, 25% were opposed, and 10% had no opinion. Overall, 45% favoured individual compensation, and 18% favoured a foundation or monument for the community at large. These figures indicated that the NAJC's educational campaign was reasonably successful.

Almost a year after the settlement, another poll showed that 76% approved of the acknowledgement and only 15% disapproved. Approval for the compensation package was 52%, with 34% disapproving, and 14% having no opinion.

Of 681 respondents in the second poll who were asked why they approved or disapproved, only 21% thought the compensation package was too generous, and 13% believed that it was not generous enough. Only 12% thought Japanese Canadians did not deserve compensation.

Both polls involved about 2,000 respondents and were conducted by Environics Research Group of Toronto. The 1986 poll results were purchased for the NAJC by the Toronto Ad Hoc Committee for Japanese Canadian Redress, and the second was commissioned by the Laurier Institute, a national non-profit organization formed in Vancouver in 1989 to sponsor research related to Canada's cultural diversity.

roots Japanese Canadians came to its defense. This internal awakening would provide the NAJC with the confidence and support—as well as the financial resources—needed to form a community position on redress.

By the spring of 1986, when there was no hope that Jelinek would ever agree to negotations with the NAJC, two major projects were completed that would become the basis for the NAJC's proposed settlement package. In March-April 1986, a questionnaire distributed in various Japanese Canadian centres indicated the community's preferences on forms of compensation. And in May 1986, the Price Waterhouse report, *Economic Losses of Japanese Canadians After 1941*, was released to the Canadian public.

By then, it had begun to appear that the government had retreated from any threat of a unilaterally imposed settlement. It may even have been at this same time that the government began reconsidering their position against a negotiated settlement. In the two years since Prime Minister Mulroney's pre-election commitment to compensate Japanese Canadians, support for redress by the Canadian public had grown steadily. In March 1986 an Environics poll revealed that 63 percent of Canadians favoured redress, and of those, 71 percent supported individual compensation.

City Councils Support Redress

TORONTO
In May 1985, The Mayor's Committee On Community Race Relations in Toronto unanimously passed a motion recommending that the federal government apologize to Japanese Canadians for the wartime injustices and establish a community foundation as part of the settlement. They also granted $5,000 to the NAJC for research on the economic losses suffered by Japanese Canadians.

The support came at a time when the NAJC was desperate for financial assistance. However, the assistance was delayed by two months when Jack Oki, Chair of the Toronto Japanese Canadian Citizens' Association (JCCA) Redress Committee wrote a letter objecting to the grant, claiming he spoke on behalf of twenty-five Japanese Canadian organizations in Toronto. At the May meeting at City Hall, NAJC supporters Dr. Wesley Fujiwara and Bill Kobayashi testified that of the twenty-one organizations which they were able to contact, not one had approved of the Toronto JCCA opposition to the grant for the NAJC's educational work.

VANCOUVER
In March 1986, Vancouver City Council granted $5,000 to the Greater Vancouver Japanese Canadian Citizens' Association (JCCA) for educational activities on redress—and unanimously passed a motion asking the federal government to negotiate a redress settlement with the NAJC, including an acknowledgement, compensation, and legislative measures to prevent a recurrence.

LETHBRIDGE
In June 1986, Lethbridge City Council granted $500 to support redress. Prior to the mass uprooting of Japanese Canadians in 1942, there was a Japanese Canadian presence in southern Alberta, primarily immigrants from the Okinawa area. Although this group was not uprooted and dispossessed, they had to register and carry ID cards, and they could not travel without permission. They were also prohibited from entering the 100-mile coastal zone.

Manitoba Government Supports Redress

Only one province officially supported redress. In Manitoba the legislature endorsed the Manitoba Intercultural Council in their call for an apology and tangible compensation. The Council, representing about fifty ethnocultural groups, is an elected advisory body to the provincial government. At the time, Ontario and BC, when approached for support, took a neutral position by saying that redress was a purely federal matter.

During 1985-86, redress for Japanese Canadians had gained prominence as an issue through the public support of many individual Canadians, organizations, and even city councils, a sign that the NAJC's educational campaign was beginning to work. More and more Canadians began to understand the value of redress as a human rights initiative.

IN 1942 CANADA SENT A LOT OF KIDS TO CAMP

You were born in Canada. Your parents were Canadian citizens. But that didn't stop the government.

Family property was seized and sold for a fraction of its worth. Your father was assigned to forced labour. You and your mother were transported to flimsy tarpaper shacks in the middle of nowhere, and left to cope with —30° winters.

Because you were a Canadian of Japanese descent, this would be your life for the next four years.

This, you discovered, was Canadian "democracy" at work.

WAS IT NECESSARY?

Were these drastic measures implemented against some 22,000 men, women and children necessary for national security?

The RCMP produced strong evidence to the contrary, but were overruled by the government.

Two tragic years later, this same government would publicly admit that no act of subversion by a single Japanese Canadian had ever been found before or during the war.

THE WRONG REMAINS

After the war they were left with little but the feeble utterances of succeeding governments. And for 41 years nothing's changed.

The present government proposes a unilateral quick fix in the name of "Multiculturalism" that does nothing to redress the real injuries suffered by these Canadians of Japanese ancestry.

It is time to right the wrong once and for all. Time, in the eyes of the world, to redress this long-standing failure of Canadian democracy itself.

WHAT YOU CAN DO

Join us in petitioning the Government of Canada to: (1) negotiate solely with the National Association of Japanese Canadians, the community's elected voice for over 38 years, (2) formally acknowledge government wrongs during and after WW II, (3) establish a just formula for compensation, and (4) insure through appropriate legislation that no future government can similarly mistreat another minority.

RIGHT THE WRONG
Support Japanese Canadian Redress

Please sign this ad and send it to:
The Canadian Council of Churches
40 St. Clair Ave. East
Toronto, Ont. M4T 1M9
It will accompany our formal petition to Ottawa.
Toronto Ad Hoc Committee for Japanese Canadian Redress.

X _B.A. Woodruff_

A tax-deductible donation toward the cost of this ad would also be greatly appreciated. Please make cheque payable to "Canadian Council of Churches (Redress)."

NAJC ANNOUNCES A DETAILED REDRESS SETTLEMENT PROPOSAL

The NAJC's educational campaign during 1985-86 was transformed into a redress position at a crucial meeting in Winnipeg, on May 17-19, 1986. With the Price Waterhouse study and the questionnaire completed, the NAJC had finally designed a "just and honourable" settlement proposal that represented the aspirations and the attitudes of Japanese Canadians. In the tense atmosphere of a crowded press conference, Art Miki and other members of the NAJC Council presented the details of a Redress Settlement Proposal.

No one was surprised when Otto Jelinek dismissed the Price Waterhouse study as irrelevant for redress discussions, and later also rejected the NAJC's Redress Settlement Proposal. Like Murta before him, Jelinek remained inflexible in ruling out individual compensation—which in effect ruled out the negotiation process with the NAJC.

The views of mainstream Canadians were reflected by the formation in Toronto of the Ad Hoc Committee for Japanese Canadian Redress, a group advocating a negotiated settlement. The Ad Hoc Committee worked to stir public awareness through a large advertisement on redress in the Globe and Mail, *March 6, 1986, paid for through individual contributors whose names were printed at the bottom of the page.*

NAJC REDRESS PROPOSAL

Submitted to the Federal Government May 20, 1986.

RECOMMENDATION 1: That an official acknowledgement of the injustices inflicted on Canadians of Japanese ancestry during and after World War II be issued by the Parliament of Canada.

RECOMMENDATION 2: That citizenship be restored to Japanese Canadians who were expelled from Canada through the government's "repatriation policy," and that the offer of citizenship should also be extended to their children.

RECOMMENDATION 3: That the records of those Japanese Canadians who were convicted under the War Measures Act be cleared.

RECOMMENDATION 4: That each living Japanese Canadian who was affected by the injustices during and after World War II be compensated $25,000.

RECOMMENDATION 5: That the Japanese Canadian community be awarded $50 million to establish a community-controlled fund to undertake projects and activities that strengthen its social and cultural well-being.

RECOMMENDATION 6: That the War Measures Act be amended in such a manner as to ensure that similar injustices will not recur, and further that a serious commitment be made to initiate a review and amendment of the Charter of Rights and Freedoms to guarantee that the rights of individuals will never again be abrogated on the basis of ancestry.

RECOMMENDATION 7: That a Japanese Canadian Human Rights Foundation be established to foster human rights. Such a foundation could provide:

- assistance to groups who are targets of racism and whose rights have been violated

- grants for research against racism and prejudice

- development of educational materials on the experience of Japanese Canadians

- organizing national and international conferences, seminars and workshops on human rights issues

- participation in multicultural activities and projects

- scholarships to further intercultural understanding

The NAJC Redress Proposal announced in May 1986, reproduced from the 16-page pamphlet, Justice in Our Time (NAJC, 1988). During the spring of 1988, in the final phase of the NAJC's redress campaign, 3,000 copies were printed for wide distribution.

Norman Oikawa: 1914-1990

Nisei Norm Oikawa, from Hamilton, believed passionately in the NAJC's campaign for justice. A tireless community worker, he gave countless hours to redress work in Hamilton and surrounding areas. During a time when the NAJC was struggling desperately to gain support in the Japanese Canadian community, he travelled door-to-door visiting 1,700 Japanese Canadian homes in southwestern Ontario to promote the NAJC's efforts and to solicit donations for the movement.

Norm lived through the internment years and never forgot the suffering caused by

Norm Oikawa, talking with Sergio Marchi and John Turner, at the Ottawa Rally, April 1988.
Photo: Gordon King.

by the government's insidious "repatriation" scheme:

"There was tension [in Tashme], all kinds of tension. I remember I went to see a few families, where the kids knew about the situation, and they didn't want to go to Japan. If the

Norm Oikawa, far left, at Tashme, recounting his experiences there, on the NAJC tour of internment centres, May 1987.
Photo: Tamio Wakayama.

the government's unjust policies. While passing by the site where the camp Tashme was located, he recalled the turmoil generated

kids were under 16 they had to go to Japan with the parents. I remember some of the kids coming to me. They came crying

with tears in their eyes, asking us to stop their parents from going back to Japan. And you know, it was very very tearful for me too sometimes—I cried my eyes out, you know, to listen to these people, asking us to do some-thing about it" *(Spirit of Redress* [JC Publications, 1989], p. 124).

It was Norm's compassion and his belief in democracy that inspired other, younger Japanese Canadians. After the settlement, the NAJC recognized his outstanding contribution by presenting him with a Redress Award.

Norm Oikawa embodied the very spirit of redress that sustained the NAJC throughout the years of struggle.

BREAKDOWN OF TALKS WITH GOVERNMENT

THE THIRD MINISTER FOR REDRESS OFFERS HOPE

Otto Jelinek had failed to convince Canadians that he was capable of reaching a meaningful settlement with the Japanese Canadian community. In the final days of his work as Minister of State for Multiculturalism, he was characterized as insensitive to the human rights nature of redress, and one newspaper even dubbed him the "Rambo" minister for his bullying tactics.

When David Crombie replaced Jelinek in July 1986, there was a sense of relief in the air. The tough guy approach was gone. Crombie appeared open, candid, congenial, and sympathetic to the injustices suffered by Japanese Canadians. Some NAJC advisors believed that if there were to be any hope of a settlement with the Conservative government, this "red Tory," fresh from Indian Affairs where he had started some positive reforms, could carry it through.

In sharp contrast to the rigid formality of meetings with Otto Jelinek, the first contact with Crombie, on October 4, 1986, occurred over dinner in a private room of a restaurant off Yonge Street in Toronto. Attending this "informal" discussion for the NAJC were Art Miki, Roy Miki, and Roger Obata. Crombie appeared with Ron Doering, a lawyer who had moved with him from Indian Affairs and who was his political Chief of Staff. With no other ministerial staff members present, it seemed Crombie's strategy was to be personal and direct—no red tape to get through.

The new Minister said that he would not impose an unreasonable time limit, but that he wanted a resolution by the spring of 1987. He recognized the value of redress as a citizenship issue, and agreed

Where's the fire?

Multiculturalism Minister Otto Jelinek's impatience to settle the issue of compensation for Japanese Canadians for the mistreatment they suffered during the Second World War is insensitive if not insulting.

Why is Mr. Jelinek in such a hurry? And who is he to set deadlines and accuse the National Association of Japanese Canadians of dragging their feet?

It is the Japanese Canadian community, not the federal government, that has spent 43 years waiting for wrongs to be righted. If feet have been dragged they are not Japanese Canadian feet. So if the NAJC prefers to wait two months for completion of a study before putting forward its position on compensation, why should the government object?

In threatening to bypass the NAJC and negotiate with smaller Japanese Canadian groups, Mr. Jelinek is behaving like a frustrated employer dealing with a stubborn union. But this is not some hard-nosed labor negotiation. It is Canada trying to make up for abusing the rights of some of its own citizens a long time ago.

The NAJC has commissioned the accounting firm of Price Waterhouse to assess the losses Japanese Canadians suffered when they were interned and their property was confiscated. The study is expected to be completed by April.

Mr. Jelinek says some of the older survivors of the wartime camps are anxious for the government to act quickly on redress. But surely they do not object to waiting another two months to make sure it is done right.

NAJC president Art Miki says the study is not intended to form the basis of a compensation claim, but to show how much the Japanese Canadian community has suffered. Fair enough. That is something all Canadians should know: the magnitude and scope of their country's mistake.

Mr. Jelinek has been quoted as saying he has been "trying to find out what use the Price Waterhouse report would be at all." If he can't figure that out for himself, he is in the wrong job.

Vancouver Sun, *January 30, 1986, one of many editorials in Canadian newspapers criticizing Otto Jelinek's handling of the Japanese Canadian redress issue.*

Veterans For and Against Redress

In April 1985, the Ontario Command of the Royal Canadian Legion passed a resolution against redress, contending that the internment of Japanese Canadians was a necessary security measure because of probable spies and collaborators in their community.

The motion was supported by a majority of the 1,300 delegates at the convention, but not all were in favour. The *Toronto Star* reported that one delegate, Roy Kennett, was outraged by the internment of Masumi Mitsui, a decorated World War I veteran and former president of a Vancouver Legion Branch. "I don't care about the traitors that fought on the Japanese side," Kennett commented, "but I do care about Mitsui and people like him." Another veteran wrote to the *Globe and Mail* on May 30, 1985 that he had resigned from the Legion because of their stand. Canadian veteran Jack Rose, contacted the Vancouver JCCA Redress Committee to offer assistance. He spoke out publicly in favour of redress as a human rights issue and subsequently became an active member of the National Coalition for Japanese Canadian Redress.

> *"A group of people were considered guilty of subversion. They were never given a chance to prove their innocence. This unfortunate incident took place over 45 years ago. But as a human being, I am most concerned about the rights of freedom and disposal of personal property which was taken away from Canadian people, living in Canada by the Canadian government without just cause or reason."*
>
> *Jack Rose, a veteran imprisoned in Hong Kong by the Japanese military, speaking at a Redress Rally in Vancouver, March 1988; from "This Week's Questions,"* The West Ender, *Vancouver, March 17, 1988.*

> *"The Japanese Canadians who were taken from their British Columbia homes and interned did not beat up Canadians in prison camps nor starve them. They were never responsible even remotely for the policy of the Japanese government nor for the actions of the Japanese armed forces nor for the administration of the prison camps. The habit of mind which flings all people of Japanese ancestry into one corner of the mind and blames them all for the crimes of some is a racist habit of mind. It begins in error and ends in injustice."*
>
> *From an editorial, "Separate Injustices,"* Winnipeg Free Press, *May 12, 1986.*

Hong Kong Vets

In 1986, Clifford Chadderton, Grand Patron of the Hong Kong Veterans of Canada Association, said that no Hong Kong veterans' organizations opposed redress, but he did ask the federal government to suspend consideration of redress to Japanese Canadians until the Japanese government indicated their intention to pay Canadian veterans for their slave labour.

Although the opposition of some veterans threatened the NAJC's cause, the controversy helped to dramatize the mistreatment of Japanese Canadians during the 1940s. Those who could not see the difference between Canadians of Japanese ancestry and Japanese nationals were reinforcing the very racist perceptions that were endorsed by the government's internment policy. The Canadian soldiers, particularly the Hong Kong veterans who were subject to torture by the Japanese military, were the victims of warfare; the civilian Canadians of Japanese ancestry who were uprooted and dispossessed in this country were the victims of a breakdown in Canadian democracy. The injustices were not comparable—and in comparing them, the veterans opposed to redress failed to recognize the human rights issue at stake for Japanese Canadians. Indeed, redress affirmed those very democratic rights that Canada fought for in World War II.

Roger Obata

In 1945, a Toronto nisei group, the Japanese Canadian Committee for Democracy (JCCD), lobbied the government to allow Japanese Canadians to enlist in the armed forces. Roger Obata, an executive member of the JCCD recalled:

"The issue of volunteering for the armed services came up in Toronto, when we had a mass meeting at the Church of All Nations. You can imagine at that time—this was in late 1943—there was still a lot of bitterness among the people who were relocated about the way Japanese Canadians were treated. So when we, as the Japanese Canadian Committee for Democracy, got up on the platform and advocated enlistment in the armed services, we weren't very popular. But I think many of the leaders of that time realized that eventually we were going to be faced with this question of Redress and having our rights justified, you know, having justice done to our experiences during the war period. So even in those days I think Redress was in the back of the minds of a lot of the people who joined up in the army....When the meeting voted against joining up, then we as an executive all resigned en masse,

and the whole executive joined up within the week. And that's how we all got into the army" (*Spirit of Redress* [JC Publications, 1989], p. 133).

After graduating from S-20, the Japanese language school division of the Canadian army's Intelligence Corps, Sergeant Obata was stationed in Washington, DC, translating Japanese wartime documents. In 1946, he returned to Toronto and worked with the Co-operative Committee for Japanese Canadians, a broad-based coalition of Canadians that was successful in pressuring the government to withdraw its "deportation" policy. He was a founding member of the National Japanese Canadian Citizens' Association in 1947, and became its first president.

As the decades slipped by in silence, Roger continued to nurture a desire for redress to resolve the "unfinished business" of the wartime injustices. In 1977 Roger, as president of the Japanese Canadian Centennial Society, helped initiate a renewed interest in the issues raised by the internment.

When the NAJC's redress movement gained momentum in the early 1980s, he assumed a vital role in the struggle, often working to attract other nisei who

had previously preferred to remain silent about the wartime injustices.

As a senior nisei who gave a lifetime of work to the politics of the Japanese Canadian community, Roger helped provide the invaluable bridge between the past and the present.

Roger served as Vice-President of the NAJC (1985-88) and became a member of the NAJC's Strategy Committee that negotiated the historic redress settlement.

In 1991 Roger became a Member of the Order of Canada.

> *"Is the Legion saying that Canadian citizens of Japanese descent were all enemies of Canada during World War II? Are they unable to differentiate between the true enemy and citizens of Canada? "Why would we have served in the armed services of Canada had it not been for our loyalty to Canada? How many Canadians would have volunteered for the armed forces while their families were incarcerated in concentration camps. Let's be fair about this."*
>
> Roger Obata, from a letter to the editor, Toronto Star, *April 17, 1985.*

(top) **David Crombie, second from left, with his Chief of Staff, Ron Doering, far left, meeting with the Vancouver JCCA Redress Committee, Japanese Language School, January 1987.**

Photo: Tony Tamayose.

(above) **NAJC Council members at a meeting in Vancouver, May 1987, from left to right: Mas Terakita and Jerry Hisaoka from Lethbridge, Fumi Ono from Kelowna, and Ken Noma from Toronto.**

Photo: Connie Kadota.

with the concept of an official acknowledgement of the injustices. As for compensation, he said the government favoured some form of a group settlement fund, but he left open the issue of who would control the fund: the government or the NAJC.

The dinner meeting ended amiably—and with some degree of optimism.

CROMBIE PROMISES A PROCESS

By the fall of 1986, the Negotiation Team, which had been specifically formed to work with Jack Murta, was dissolved, and in its place the NAJC Council established a Strategy Committee both to advise the Council on how to proceed and to plan the future course of the redress movement.

This NAJC Strategy Committee first met with David Crombie and Ron Doering in Toronto on November 22, 1986, at which time Crombie announced his intent to make a recommendation to the Prime Minister on both a procedure to arrive at a settlement and the elements of a redress package.

Although aware of the NAJC's Redress Proposal of May 1986, and the Redress Questionnaire showing support for compensation in a combined individual and community form, Crombie asked for time to meet privately with some individuals and groups in the Japanese Canadian community. As he explained, he wanted to understand redress personally, so that his recommendations would be based on face-to-face discussions with those directly affected by the injustices.

The NAJC had opposed similar requests by Murta and Jelinek to "consult" with individual Japanese Canadians directly, but Crombie's easy going manner, and his apparent desire to work with the NAJC, were effective manoeuvers on his part. The NAJC agreed to his request, pulled back, and waited.

CROMBIE CONSULTS WITH JAPANESE CANADIANS

Crombie began by meeting with a few "high-profile" individual Japanese Canadians of his choice to listen to their personal views on redress, although he remarked that he would also talk with ordinary Japanese Canadians, such as his dry cleaner. He spoke with Tom Shoyama, former Deputy Minister of Finance, Joy Kogawa (author of *Obasan*), Ken Adachi (author of *The Enemy That Never Was*), and Toronto architect Raymond Moriyama whose work includes the Japanese Canadian Cultural Centre in Toronto, Toronto's Science Centre, and the Metro Toronto Library.

Responding to pressure to include the west in his personal consultations, Crombie made one visit to Vancouver. On January 16, 1987, he met with the Greater Vancouver Japanese Canadian Citizens' Association (JCCA) in the historic Japanese Language School on Alexander Street, in the very area that was the original site of the mass uprooting in 1942. There, already some five months after assuming responsibility for redress, he reiterated that he would soon recommend—he "hoped" in February—a process to reach a settlement.

By then, however, his credibility amongst Japanese Canadians was beginning to wane. In his Vancouver meeting he was evasive, vague, and uncommitted when asked about the real issue—compensation to individuals who had suffered injustices and who were still alive. There were no signs that his position would differ substantially from his predecessors.

NAJC GOES TO OTTAWA TO LOBBY

Uneasy with Crombie's lack of action and commitment, the NAJC Strategy Committee met for three days in March 1987. The plan was not only to map out strategy in the now likely event that Crombie would reject the NAJC's

Japanese Canadian leaving Hastings Park after giving up his car to the government, 1942. Photo: Vancouver Public Library #1378.

Art Miki, NAJC President, at NAJC Press Conference in Vancouver, May 17, 1987, rejecting the government's offer in a letter to David Crombie: "We are shocked to learn that after considering this issue for nine months, and being aware of the enormity of the losses involved, you could recommend to the Government that an amount in the range of $12 million could represent a fair and just settlement of our claim."

Photo: Tamio Wakayama.

Redress Proposal, but also to establish contacts with various government and opposition figures to promote the concept of a negotiation process.

Meetings were arranged with John Fraser (Speaker of the House), Cliff Chadderton (Patron of the Hong Kong War Veterans Association), Ernie Epp (NDP Multiculturalism critic), Sergio Marchi (Liberal Multiculturalism critic), Dalton Camp (advisor to the Prime Minister) and Don Mazankowski (Deputy Prime Minister).

Meanwhile, the NAJC waited for Crombie's redress proposal.

CROMBIE OFFERS A COMMUNITY FUND, BUT NO NEGOTIATIONS

The long-awaited response from Crombie came as a major disappointment. After promising a meaningful process, he sent the NAJC yet another "take-it-or-leave-it" offer, outlined in his official letter, dated March 27, 1987:

- an official Acknowledgement of injustices
- a review of the War Measures Act
- a $12 million community fund to heal the community and redress the wrongs.

The principle of individual compensation had been rejected again.

CROMBIE REMAINS INFLEXIBLE

On May 8, 1987, the NAJC Strategy Committee flew to Ottawa to plead with Crombie for a negotiation process on all the elements of the NAJC's Redress Proposal, including individual compensation.

There was no flexibility in the $12 million figure. Crombie repeatedly insisted that his offer represented what he termed his government's largest "footprint."

Crombie's position differed from Jelinek's in two ways: the monetary figure had risen, from

$10 to $12 million; and he was willing to grant the NAJC control over the funds—which perhaps may have been negotiable with Jelinek had the NAJC wanted to settle on that basis. Most crucially, however, he had taken a public position against direct compensation to individuals. His suggestion that the NAJC could divide the community fund among individuals was insulting, since this would result in a mere $850 for each of the estimated 14,000 surviving victims.

NAJC COUNCIL REJECTS CROMBIE'S OFFER

The NAJC Council formally rejected Combie's offer at a conference held May 16-18, 1987 in Vancouver. Speaking on behalf of the NAJC, President Art Miki issued a strongly worded letter to Crombie, criticizing his failure to recommend a process acceptable to Japanese Canadians:

> We maintain our position that a just settlement must acknowledge each affected person as an individual, not merely as a member of an ethnic group. Your proposal fails to acknowledge that injustices were suffered by individuals, some 14,000 of whom are still alive.
>
> ...Our claim is based upon losses of civil rights, property and human dignity that have never been justified in terms of military security, and that illustrate the essentially racist nature of the government's actions. A settlement offer that amounts to approximately $50 per affected individual in 1945 dollars belittles the significance of the issue. You, like the Ministers before you, have failed to fulfill the promise made by Mr. Mulroney in May 1984, to compensate Japanese Canadians (From a letter to David Crombie, May 17, 1987).

Group leaving for a tour of the internment camps in the BC interior, following the NAJC Conference, Vancouver, May 1987. The site of the departure, the Japanese Language School, was left by the Custodian for community meetings during the uprooting. It remains the only prewar community facility still used by Japanese Canadians.
Photo: Tamio Wakayama.

105

Kathleen Hayami from Montreal and Bill Kobayashi from Toronto, both NAJC Council members, at the NAJC Conference in Vancouver, May 1987.
Photo: Connie Kadota.

Miki's letter concluded with a request to meet with Prime Minister Brian Mulroney.

TALKS WITH CROMBIE END

Shortly after the NAJC Council rejected Crombie's offer, on June 1, 1987, the Strategy Committee met with Crombie in Ottawa, in one last effort to have him reconsider his position—but he remained inflexible.

The last contact with Crombie took place the next month, on July 11, 1987, in Winnipeg. There the Minister made it clear that he opposed individual compensation because he did not believe Japanese Canadians were entitled to it. They had suffered due to the war, but everyone in Canada had suffered, he said. He also rejected the NAJC's argument that redress be based upon the injustices inflicted on Canadians because of their racial ancestry. His adviser, lawyer Ron Doering, pointed out that the NAJC did not have a legal claim, only a moral one. In other words, since the abuses of Japanese Canadians were legal under the War Measures Act, the government today was not responsible for compensating individuals.

By the end of this meeting, Crombie confirmed that $12 million was his government's best—and final—offer. There would be no negotiation process.

Crombie concluded by saying he would report to the Prime Minister that discussions on redress with the NAJC would now terminate.

AFTER CROMBIE

The complete breakdown of talks with Crombie had an immediate demoralizing effect on Japanese Canadians, who had placed high hopes in his apparently sympathetic approach. Now that three ministers had failed to resolve redress, many in the community began to lose faith in the movement. Some were even disturbed that the NAJC had not accepted the $12 million offer. Cynicism crept into the discussions: Isn't $12 million better than nothing?

Crombie's nine months of stalling tactics had weakened the NAJC's campaign, but only temporarily. What appeared to be a dead end, from another perspective, was simply the beginning of another phase.

Without intending to do so, Crombie helped bring into public perspective the principle of justice and human rights on which the NAJC had built its entire redress program. In defending his rejection of individual compensation, he had reasoned that Japanese Canadians were interned as a community, so compensation should be made in group form. In effect, he was espousing the very injustice that lay behind the government's actions in 1942. At that time, the individual citizenship rights of a group of innocent Canadians had been violated merely on the basis of a common racial ancestry.

Crombie's position embodied an obvious logical flaw which brought into focus the value of recognizing individuals in a redress settlement. How could a government that acknowledged the violation of individual rights not offer compensation on that same basis? Indeed, how could a group be compensated for injustices suffered by individuals? Unwittingly, then, Crombie had created a climate for the first real public debate on the principle of individual compensation.

It was in the aftermath of the NAJC's conflicts with Crombie that public opinion came to favour the NAJC's position, not only on the question of a negotiated settlement, but also on the basis for such a negotiated settlement: individual compensation.

Why Individual and Community Compensation?

The principle of compensation to individuals remained the greatest obstacle in the NAJC's discussions with the government. Each of the ministers, with the exception of Gerry Weiner, opposed this element in the NAJC's redress proposal. For the NAJC, however, a just and honourable settlement had to recognize the individual. After all, the injustices of the 1940s resulted when the government violated the rights of individuals and branded them "enemy alien" merely on the basis of their racial ancestry. It was the individual who consequently suffered the loss of freedom, confiscation of property and belongings, the forced dispersal away from the coast, and even exile from this country.

On the other hand, the mass uprooting destroyed the Japanese Canadian community on the west coast where over 95 percent of the population lived before 1942. Along with businesses and properties, facilities such as community halls, churches, and schools were confiscated and sold by the Custodian of Enemy Property. The government's dispersal policy "east of the Rockies" in the spring of 1945, when the end of the war was in sight, was designed to prevent Japanese Canadians from returning to the coast to rebuild their community. This forced assimilation in effect meant that Japanese Canadians lost the community ties that they enjoyed before 1942.

It was because the injustices directly affected both the individual and the community, that the NAJC sought compensation in both forms.

COMMUNITY ACTION—
NAJC SEEKS SUPPORT OF CANADIANS

RESOLUTION

In Support of Japanese Canadian Redress
Multicultural Rally
Harbord Collegiate Institute
Toronto, Thursday, October 29, 1987

We, the undersigned national organizations representing Canadians of diverse ethnocultural heritage, hereby call upon the Prime Minister to intervene personally to resolve this basic human and civil rights issue.

We urge the Prime Minister to act swiftly to heal this wound on our national psyche and, thereby, to reinforce for all Canadians their faith in the accountability of parliamentary democracy.

The Korean Canadian Cultural Associa-
tion of Metropolitan Toronto
International Sikh Organization—
Federation of Sikh Societies
Council of Muslim Communities of
Canada
United Council of Filipino Associations
in Canada
Pakistani Canadian Community Center
(Toronto) Inc.
Hellenic Canadian Congress

German Canadian Congress
National Council of Jamaicans
Canadian Lithuanian Community
National Congress of Italian Canadians
Chinese Canadian National Council
Canadian Arab Federation
Canadian Polish Congress
Canadian Jewish Congress
Canadian Hispanic Congress
Czechoslovak Association of Canada

"Resolution" endorsed by national ethnic organizations at the Multicultural Rally in Toronto, October 29, 1987; reproduced from the pamphlet, Justice in Our Time *(NAJC, 1988).*

> " *The day has passed when Japanese Canadians will fall alone.* "
>
> *Michael Czuma, Polish Canadian Congress, Multicultural Rally, Toronto, October 29, 1987.*

In the fall of 1987, as the NAJC entered the fourth year of the redress campaign, the prospect of a quick, negotiated settlement had faded. Financial resources were dwindling and many individuals who had once enthusiastically supported the cause were drawing back into their private lives.

In one more attempt to rejuvenate public interest in the cause, the NAJC decided to use most of the remaining funds to seek broad-based support for a negotiated settlement, including direct compensation to the Japanese Canadians interned. A blueprint was drawn for the formation of a national coalition of individuals and groups who collectively would represent mainstream Canadians. A series of rallies was planned in major NAJC centres, which would culminate in a massive rally on Parliament Hill the following spring.

At the first rally, the "Multicultural Rally" at Harbord Collegiate in Toronto on October 29, 1987, the NAJC received an impressive demonstration of support from fifteen national ethnic organizations. Representatives spoke out in sympathy for Japanese Canadians whose rights had been violated during the 1940s and called on the government to negotiate a meaningful settlement with the NAJC. Their support was reinforced in the form of a signed petition, establishing a model for what became the National Coalition for Japanese Canadian Redress.

One tell-tale sign that public opinion on individual compensation was shifting came on September 17, 1987. On that day the US House of Representatives passed the Civil Liberties Bill which offered $20,000 to individual Japanese

(left) **Ethnic leaders speaking in support of the NAJC at the Multicultural Rally at Harbord Collegiate in Toronto, October 29, 1987.** *Photo: Toronto Chapter, National Association of Japanese Canadians.*

(below left) **The Toronto Japanese Canadian Cultural Centre's taiko group, Osuwa Daiko, performing at the Multicultural Rally.** *Photo: Toronto Chapter, National Association of Japanese Canadians.*

(below) **At the American Consulate rally, from left to right: Nancy Hoita, Yoe Ebisuzaki, Polly Okuna.** *Courtesy of Nancy Hoita.*

(below) **Stum Shimizu, a nisei World War II veteran, at the rally organized by the NAJC Toronto Chapter in front of the American Consulate in Toronto on August 12, 1988, a few days after US President Ronald Reagan signed the redress bill. In a twist on the**

"protest rally" format, Japanese Canadians congratulated the American government on the passage of the Japanese American redress bill and called on the Canadian government to negotiate a settlement with the NAJC. *Photo: Nancy Hoita.*

Americans who had been incarcerated in the US during World War II. Although the bill still had to get through the Senate, and then be signed by President Reagan, its passage in the House of Representatives was a beacon for the NAJC's human rights struggle in Canada. After all, the Canadian government had treated Japanese Canadians more severely than the American government had treated its citizens, and the US action affirmed redress as a civil rights issue.

Near the end of 1987, the only sign that the government might reconsider its position came on December 15, when Art Miki and NAJC representatives were invited to speak on redress before the government's Standing Committee on Multiculturalism.

Otherwise, the government had remained silent on redress.

Japanese American Redress Settlement: The Civil Liberties Act of 1987

On September 17, 1987, the House of Representatives passed the Civil Liberties Act of 1987, Bill HR442 on the 200th anniversary of the American Constitution. The Bill was named in honour of the 442nd division, the highly decorated Japanese American unit that had fought for the USA in World War II. This was the first tangible show of political support in the USA or Canada for redress to aggrieved individuals, and the Bill provided for the payment of $20,000 to each surviving internee, plus a community education fund.

The American political system differs from the Canadian one in several important aspects. First, party members vote according to their individual conscience, not on party lines. While this provides more diversity than party-line voting, it means each representative must be lobbied individually. As well, the House bill does not proceed to the Senate for consideration, but the Senate draws its own parallel, but not identical bill. Once they both pass, the two bills must be reconciled to make them compatible. The bills do not become law until signed by the President, and the rumour was that President Reagan was not in favour of redress. There were delays in bringing the Bill forward in the Senate, but it was finally approved on April 20, 1988. On August 10, 1988, President Reagan signed the Bill into law.

NEARLY EMPTY VICTORY

The compensation of $20,000 per individual was payable to those interned during the war, and alive as of August 10, 1988. Japanese Americans living outside the coastal area who were not interned were not eligible. About 64,000 people registered with the Office of Redress Administration. Unfortunately, no provisions were included in the legislation to ensure a budget to enact the settlement. Each year, the JACL lobbied for budget allocations, and finally in 1990, obtained an entitlement program which assures future funding. The first cheques were issued in a ceremony on October 9, 1990 to the six oldest recipients able to travel, all over 100 years of age.

Fumiko Hayashi and her daughter, Natalie, wearing identification tags during the uprooting of Japanese Americans from the west coast.
Photo: Library of Congress 106998-LCUSZ62-88338; names from Coming Home *(Japanese American Citizens League, 1988), p. 39.*

THE OTTAWA RALLY—PROTEST ON PARLIAMENT HILL

The gathering of Japanese Canadians in Ottawa, organized around a Redress Forum, was set for April 1988, the historic month in 1949 when the restrictions were lifted and Japanese Canadians were finally free to return to the coast. This dignified and emotionally charged gathering became the turning point in the NAJC's national campaign.

CROMBIE REPLACED BY GERRY WEINER

Just prior to the Ottawa rally, Gerry Weiner became the fourth Minister in the Conservatives' four years in power to work on redress.

In that same month, the US Senate ratified the American redress bill, a move that had not seemed possible a year before. Public opinion in the US had ultimately decided in favour of Japanese Americans. Japanese Canadians now had some reason to hope for a similar transformation of their government's attitudes.

(left) **Redress postcards being spread out at the Ottawa Forum by Hide (Hyodo) Shimizu from Toronto.** *Photo: Gordon King.*

(above) **Harry Tsuchiya from Hamilton carrying a bag of redress postcards to the Prime Minister's office. Gerry Weiner later admitted to the NAJC Strategy Committee that he had reported to Cabinet how impressed he was by the speeches at the Ottawa Forum. When thousands of yellow postcards were scattered before the speaker's podium with a message for the Prime Minister to resolve "Redress Now," Weiner offered to escort the carriers to the Prime Minister's office directly.** *Photo: Gordon King.*

(above right) **From January to March 1988, the NAJC held rallies in Montreal, Toronto, Winnipeg and Vancouver to** develop the National Coalition for Japanese Canadian Redress and to publicize their call for a negotiated settlement. It was

at such gatherings that prominent individuals and groups joined the NAJC's struggle. In this photo, John Shimizu from Vancouver Island attends a rally in Vancouver in March. His protest is a reference to "$1.49 Day," a monthly super-discount day at Woodward's, a western department store. *Photo: Peter Battistoni, Vancouver Sun.*

The National Coalition for Japanese Canadian Redress: Who Stood with Us?

The National Coalition for Japanese Canadian Redress became a powerful unifying voice for Canadians from all backgrounds who supported the redress aims of the NAJC. Ethnic organizations, church and labour groups, civil rights leaders, and many prominent individuals signed the Coalition agreement, thereby endorsing the NAJC's call for a negotiated settlement which would include a figure for individual compensation. Crombie's inflexibility on the issue of individual rights provided the ideal rallying point for the NAJC's campaign. It was the first time that widespread support for the NAJC's position on individual rights was publicly affirmed by such a large representative group. Members of the Coalition came from all parts of Canada and a wide variety of occupations. The following list was compiled from information supplied on the membership forms.

Irving Abella, *Historian,Toronto*
Johnny N. Adams, *WildlifeTechnician, Kuujjuaq PQ*
Peter Adams, *Plumber, Kuujjuaq PQ*
Tommy Adams, *T.V. Cameraman, Kuujjuaq PQ*
Howard Adelman, *Historian, Toronto*
Timothy Agg, *Administrator, Vancouver*
Joseph Agma, *Executive Assistant, Kuujjuaq PQ*
Gregory Aikins, *Naval Officer, Ottawa*
Mary Aikins, *Homemaker, Ottawa*
Milnor Alexander, *Retired Professor, Victoria*
Jane Allan, *Education Coordinator*
Ted Allan, *Writer*
Donald C. Allen, *Hospital Worker, Vancouver*
Richard Allen, *Ont. MPP, Hamilton*
Bert Almon, *Professor, Edmonton*
George Amabile, *Professor, Winnipeg*
Vivianne Amos, *Student, Ste. Therese PQ*
Bonnie Stuart Anderson, *Student, Gloucester ON*
Robert Anderson, *Professor, Burnaby BC*
Janice Andrews, *Social Worker, Ottawa*
Aputik Angnatuk, *Secretary, Kuujjuaq PQ*
Donald Antstein, *Researcher, Burnaby BC*
Denys Arcand, *Filmmaker, Montreal*
Ann Archer, *Craftsperson, Ottawa*
Robb A. Armstrong, *Truck Driver, Vancouver*
Margot Arseneau, *Social Worker, Ottawa*
Harry W. Arthurs, *Professor, North York ON*
Margaret Atwood, *Author, Toronto*
N. Autifarff, Alderman, *New Denver BC*
Pamela Avis, Student, *Edmonton*
Morton Bain, Professor, *Dorval PQ*
Donna Balkan, *Union Officer, Ottawa*
Chin Banerjee, *Professor, Port Coquitlam BC*
David Barrett, *Former Premier of BC*
Gregory Baum, *Theologian, Toronto*
Jennifer Becherel, *Researcher*
Diane Beckett, *Consultant, Ottawa*
Marie Beliveau, *Nurse, Kuujjuaq PQ*
Glen W. Bell, *Lawyer, Ottawa*
Don Bellamy, *Executive Director, Vancouver*
Brenda Belmonte, *Directress, Winnipeg*
Edward P. Belobaba, *Lawyer, Toronto*
Thomas Berger, *Lawyer, Vancouver*
Elaine Bernard, *President, BC NDP, Vancouver*
Helen Berry, *Student, Nepean ON*
Pierre Berton, *Journalist, Toronto*
Helene Berube, *Aylmer PQ*
P. Bessette-Cappelicz, *Counsellor, Orleans PQ*
Ernie Best, *Professor, Toronto*
Fiona Beveridge, *Chief Executive, Ottawa*
Merrill Beveridge, *Secretary, Ottawa*
Kanu Bhatt, *Counsellor, Ottawa*
Frances Bickerstaff, *Bookkeeper, New Westminster*
Arthur N. Bielfeld, *Rabbi, Willowdale ON*
William Blaikie, *MP, Winnipeg-Bird's Hill*
Marie-Claire Blais, *Writer, Kingsbury PQ*
Sarmen Boac, *Union Rep, Burnaby BC*
Deanne Bogdan, *Professor*
Alice Boissonneau, *Writer, Cannington ON*

Roo Borson, *Writer, Toronto*
Robert Bose, *Mayor, Surrey BC*
J.A.S. Bouchard, *Union Rep., St. Catharines ON*
Maryanne Boughner, *Civil Servant, Ottawa*
George & Angela Bowering, *Writers, Vancouver*
Marilyn Bown, *Clergy, Birtle MB*
E. Boyanowsky, *Professor, North Vancouver*
Helen Boyce, *Alderman, Vancouver*
Dwight Boyd, *Professor, Toronto*
J. Bradley, *Professor, Montreal*
A.M. Brady, *Screenwriter, Nepean ON*
Gretchen Brewin, *Mayor, Victoria*
Gail Brighton, *Alderman, New Denver BC*
Deborah J. Brin, *Rabbi, Downsview ON*
Ed Broadbent, *MP, Leader of the NDP*
Betty Bronson, *Building Technologist, Vancouver*
Bill & Betty Brooks, *Photographers, Scarborough*
Lynn Brophy, *Community Services Worker, Ottawa*
Fran Brown, *Fish Cannery Worker, Prince Rupert*
John Brown, *Store Owner, Nanaimo BC*
P.C. Brown, *Lecturer, Verdun PQ*
Peter Buitenhuis, *Professor, West Vancouver BC*
Ellen C. Bulger, *Coordinator, Ottawa*
Vicki Burkholder, *Teacher, Fraser Lake BC*
Mae Burrows, *Video Producer, Burnaby BC*
A.H. & D.J. Burt, *Retired, North Vancouver BC*
Christine Burt, *Educator, Montreal*
Harvey Burt, *Teacher*
Yessy Byl, *Lawyer, Calgary*
M. Byrne, *Government Employee, Ottawa*
Gordon Lewis Callahan, *Banker, Vancouver*
Ron Campbell, *Janitor, Burnaby BC*
Fred Candelaria, *Prof. Emeritus, N. Vancouver BC*
Gina Calleja, *Artist, Willowdale ON*
June Callwood, *Journalist, Toronto*
Cathy Cameron, *Ottawa*
Carolynn R. Campbell, *Ottawa*
Claire Campbell, *Ottawa*
Shirley G.E. Carr, *Labour Leader*
Sharon Carstairs, *Leader, Manitoba Liberals*
John Cashore, *BC MLA, Coquitlam BC*
Michael Cassidy, *MP, Ottawa Centre*
Peter C. Cavers, *Ottawa*
E.V. Cavin, *Teacher, Ottawa*
Irv Chamney, *Hotel Desk Clerk, Comox BC*
Meena Chandramouli, *Student, Ottawa*
Gloria Chao, *Student, Vancouver*
Josee Charlebois, *Horticulturist, Ottawa*
Brian Charlton, *MPP, Hamilton ON*
Laurance Chediac, *Student, St. Laurent PQ*
M. A. Chene, *Nepean ON*
Robert Cherry, *Guidance Counsellor, Aylmer PQ*
Peter Chimbos, *Greek Canadian Community Leader*
Timothy J. Christian, *Dean of Law, U. of Alberta*
Jean Christie, *Executive Director, Ottawa*
Derek Chu, *Student, Vancouver*
Barrie A. Clark, *Broadcaster, West Vancouver BC*
Glen Clark, *MLA, Vancouver BC*
Lovell C. Clark, *Retired Professor, Winnipeg*

Austin Clarke, *Author, Toronto*
Adrienne Clarkson, *Publisher, Toronto*
Murray Cliff, *Pilot, Vancouver*
Bruce Cockburn, *Musician, Ottawa*
Nicole Coderre, *Maison d'amitie, Hull PQ*
Richard Coe, *Professor, Vancouver*
Marjorie Cohen, *Economist*
Frances Combs, *United Church Minister, Toronto*
Ramsay Cook, *Historian, Toronto*
Doris Corbeil, *Custodian, Creston BC*
Donald J.M. Corbett, *College Principal, Toronto*
Roland de Corneille, *MP*
A. Costigan, *Career Counsellor, Ottawa*
Irwin Cotler, *Law Professor, Quebec, PQ*
Elizabeth Coupland, *Registered Nurse, Nepean ON*
W. J. Coupland, *Member of Armed Forces, Nepean*
Kirsten Cowan, *Student, Ottawa*
David Croll, *Senator, Toronto*
Tara Cullis, *Writer, Vancouver*
A. Cunningham, *Nurse, Nepean ON*
Karen Curran, *Educator, Carleton Place ON*
James Currie, *Executive Assistant, Victoria*
Jared Curtis, *Professor, Burnaby BC*
Arnold Dagenais, *College Administrator, Montreal W*
Antonio D'Alfonso, *Publisher, Montreal*
Manoj Das, *Manager*

> " *Injustices to Canadians on the basis of race are the saddest part of the history of Canada. We must seek to acknowledge and settle this issue in a manner satisfactory to the community that suffered. The government has an opportunity to resolve the matter now.* "
>
> *Dr. Lillian Ma, Canadian Ethnocultural Council, from the pamphlet* Justice in Our Time *(NAJC, 1988).*

Alan Davies, *Professor*

Libby Davies, *Vancouver Alderman*

Barry Davis, *Economist, Ottawa*

Peter H. Davis, *Geraldton ON*

Don E. Davison, *School Board Employee, Surrey*

Mike Davison, *Writer, Hamilton*

Karen Dean, *Union Rep, Burnaby BC*

Graeme Decarie, *Historian*

Laurence Decore, *Mayor, Edmonton*

Pascual Delgado, *Director, Montreal*

Betsie Dempsey, *Ottawa*

Robert F. Dennis, *Systems Analyst, Ottawa*

Remi De Roo, *Bishop, Roman Catholic Church, Victoria*

Wendy DesBrisay, *Adult Educator, Ottawa*

Manon Descotes, *Accounting, Ottawa*

Francis E. Devito, *Director, Fruitvale BC*

Clare Devlin, *Personnel Officer, Ottawa*

Marion Dewar, *MP, Hamilton Mountain ON*

Emma Dickson, *Instructor, Ottawa*

Ravida Din, *Student, Ottawa*

Helen Dixon, *Radio Journalist, Vancouver*

Sandra Djwa, *Chair, Dept. of English, Vancouver*

J. M. Doi, *Business Analyst, Nepean ON*

Michael Donnelly, *Professor, Toronto*

Anne Dougherty, *Mother, Ottawa*

Anne Dowson, *Radio Producer, Ottawa*

Cassie J. Doyle, *Social Worker, Ottawa*

Sandra J. Drake, *Bookkeeper, Toronto*

Thomas M. Drouillard, *Engineer, Wallaceburg ON*

Joyce Dubuc, *Computer Operator, Ottawa*

Nicholas Ducic, *Student, Montreal*

Martin Duckworth, *Filmmaker, Montreal*

Louis Dudek, *Retired Professor, Montreal*

Frances Duncan, *Writer, Gabriola BC*

Robert Dunham, *Professor, Vancouver*

Robyn Durling, *Researcher, Vancouver*

Anna Dwyer, *Broadcaster, Vancouver*

Wayne Easter, *President, National Farmers Union*

George Egerton, *Professor, Vancouver*

Arthur C. Eggleton, *Mayor, Toronto*

Margrit Eichler, *Educator, Toronto*

Dorothy Elias, *Printer, Vancouver*

Vivian W. Elkins, *Retired Teacher, Montreal*

Clifford Elliot, *Clergy, Toronto*

Kathryn Emslie, *Executive Assistant, Toronto*

Lawrence Englander, *Rabbi, Mississauga ON*

Patricia Englund, *Agrologist, Saskatoon*

Ernie Epp, *MP, Thunder Bay-Nipigon*

Georges Erasmus, *National Chief, Assembly of First Nations*

Bruce G. Eriksen, *Vancouver Alderman*

Monireh Eslami, *Nurse-Midwife, Ottawa*

Cristina Estable, *Artist, Ottawa*

Linda May Ethell, *Housewife, Nepean ON*

Lee Farnworth, *Educator, Nepean ON*

Grace Fatkin, *Teacher, Langley BC*

Debbie Ferren-Mayo, *Secretary, Ottawa*

Mark C. Feyz, *Businessman, Mississauga ON*

Ben Fiber, *Journalist, Toronto*

Fatima Filippi, *Coordinator, Rexdale ON*

Nancy Fillmore, *Student, Ottawa*

Timothy Findlay, *Author, Cannington ON*

James M. Finlay, *Retired Minister, Barrie ON*

Shirley Finter, *Artist, Ottawa*

Pam Fitzgerald, *Manager, Ottawa*

Robert Fleming, *Student, Victoria*

William Ford, *Security Agent, Kuujjuaq PQ*

Louise Fortier, *Student, Hull PQ*

Tony Foster, *Writer, Halifax*

Watson A. Fournier, *Engineer, Kuujjuaq PQ*

Edith Fowke, *Folklorist, Downsview ON*

Robert Fox, *Consultant, Ottawa*

David Franklyn-Ratchford, *Writer-Director, Scarborough ON*

Patrick Friesen *T.V. Producer, Poet, Playwright, Winnipeg*

Kathleen Frizzell, *Writer, Vancouver*

Northrop Frye, *Author, Toronto*

Robert Fulford, *Columnist, Toronto*

Betty Gordon Funke, *Writer, Victoria*

Muriel Gustavson, *Teacher, Nanaimo BC*

C.L. Furlow, *Trainer, Ottawa*

Suzanne Gagnon, *Social Worker, Ottawa*

Michelle Gagnon, *Executive Secretary, Montreal*

John A. Galko, *Manager, Nepean ON*

Ken Georgetti, *President, BC Federation of Labor*

Mario Gerbeau, *Lawyer, Kuujjuaq PQ*

Christine Gervais, *Translator, Kuujjuaq PQ*

Patricia Gibbons, *Social Worker, Quebec PQ*

Michael E. Gibbs, *Security Worker, New Westminster*

Graeme Gibson, *Author, Toronto*

William C. Gibson, *Physician, Victoria*

Greg Gigg, *Truck Driver, Vancouver*

William Gilbey, *Civil Rights Activist, Regina*

Charan Gill, *President, BCOFR*

Harry Glasbeek, *Law Professor, Toronto*

Colleen Glass, *Engineer, Ottawa*

Terry Glavin, *Reporter, New Westminster BC*

Charles Glazner, *Forest Technician, Courtenay BC*

Susan Glickman, *English Professor, Toronto*

Roxanne Goddard, *Self-employed, Vancouver*

Victor C. Goldbloom, *Physician, Montreal*

Janet Goldre, *Ottawa*

Charlie M. Gordon, *Kuujjuaq PQ*

Martha Gordon, *Clerk, Kuujjuaq PQ*

Tommy S. Gordon, *General Manager*

Willie Gordon, *Negotiator, Kuujjuaq PQ*

Jerry Grafstein, *Senator, Toronto*

Charles C. Gray, *Musician*

Mary Gray, *ESL Instructor, Ottawa*

Mark Greenwald, *College Professor, Vankleek Hill ON*

Dale Greer, *Mother, Ottawa*

Frances Gregory, *Lawyer, Toronto*

Michelle Gregory, *Student, Ottawa*

Thomas Grieve, *University Teacher, Mission BC*

Dennis Grimolfson, *Engineering Aide, Winnipeg*

Norman Grist, *Heavy Equipment Operator, Kuujjuaq*

Terry Gronbeck-Jones, *Student, Ottawa*

Irene Grondin, *Proofreader, Ottawa*

Normand Grondin, *Member of Armed Forces, Ottawa*

Susi Grudo, *Mother, Ottawa*

Louise Guenette, *Coordinator, Ottawa*

Paul Guenette, *Camera Operator, Vancouver*

Francine Guertin, *Travailleuse Sociale, Gatineau PQ*

Muriel Gustavson, *Teacher, Nanaimo*

P. Habmixay, *Assureur-vie, Quebec*

Dustie Halmai, *Homemaker*

Ella Hamilton, *Counsellor, Balderson ON*

John B. Hamilton, *Retired, Winnipeg*

Vera Hamilton, *Clerk, New Denver BC*

Wilma Hamilton, *Real Estate Agent, Winnipeg*

Michael Harcourt, *BC MLA, Vancouver*

Suzanne Harding, *Homemaker, Ottawa*

Gus Harris, *Mayor, Scarborough ON*

Mason Harris, *Professor, North Vancouver*

A. Hart, *Retired Nurse, Victoria*

Don Harvey, *Engineer, Gloucester ON*

Hanny A. Hassan, *Engineer, London ON*

Maral Hassessian, *Student, Montreal*

Beata Hasznik, *Artist*

James Hathaway, *Law Professor*

David W. Hawthorne, *Civil Servant, Ottawa*

Diana Hawthorne, *Labour Affairs Officer, Vancouver*

H.A.B. Hawthorne, *North Vancouver BC*

Mary F. Hawthorne, *Nurse, Ottawa*

Dan Heap, *MP, Spadina ON*

Paul Hedlin, *Teacher, Montreal*

Cathy Henderson, *TWU Human Rights Officer, Burnaby*

Debra Henderson, *Film Executive*

Nel Henteleff, *Homemaker, Dugald MB*

Paul D. Henteleff, *Physician, Dugald MB*

Peter Herrndorf, *Publisher Toronto Life Magazine*

Philip Hewett, *Clergy*

George Heyman, *Union Officer, BCGEU*

Doreen Hierlihy, *Proofreader, Ottawa*

Arthur Hiess, *Dir., Canadian Inst. of Minority Rights*

Jean Higginson, *Librarian, Ottawa*

Daisy Lloyd Highfield, *Retired, Scarborough ON*

Esther Mary Highfield, *Retired, Scarborough ON*

Frances M. Hill, *Homemaker, Ottawa*

James K. Hill, *Instructor, Regina*

Brian Hinkley, *Alderman, City of Hamilton*

Carroll Holland, *Journalist, Ottawa*

Heather Holubowich, *Medical Secretary, Ottawa*

Margaret Holubowich, *Real Estate Broker, Nepean*

Meg Hopkins, *Nurses Aide, Burnaby BC*

Maya Houssami, *Student, Ottawa*

Lyndell A. Hughes, *Retired, Ottawa*

Thomas J. Hughes, *Student, Fort Langley BC*

M.E. Huis, *Union Rep, Vancouver*

Wendy Hunt, *Adult Educator*

Mel Hurtig, *Publisher, Edmonton*

Carol Husband, *Ottawa*

Jean Hutcheon, *Computer Worker, Kanata ON*

Pat Hutchings, *Lawyer, Sidney BC*

George Ignatieff, *President, Science for Peace*

Brian Iler, *Solicitor, Toronto*

Paul I. Irwin, *United Church Minister, Scarborough*

Barbara Jackman, *Lawyer, Toronto*

Wendy James, *Social Worker, Chelsea PQ*

Pat Jeeves, *Social Worker, Carleton Place ON*

Pauline Jewett, *MP, New Westminster-Coquitlam BC*

Shell Johanson, *Businessman, Don Mills ON*

Donna F. Johnson, *Social Worker, Kanata ON*

Barry Jones, *BC MLA, Burnaby BC*

John T. Jones, *Teacher, Kamloops BC*

Colleen Jordan, *Library Technician, Burnaby BC*

James J. Kafieh, *Businessman, Winnipeg*

David Kai, *Minister, Birtle MB*

Robyn Kall, *Computer Analyst, Ottawa*

Kulman Kaplansky, *Human Rights Centre, University of Ottawa*

Joseph Katz, *Educator, Vancouver*

Norma Kavanagh, *Domestic Engineer, Kanata ON*

Janice Kulyk Keefer, *Writer, Annapolis Royal NS*

Cyril Keeper, *MP, Winnipeg North Centre*

Anthony Keith, *Lawyer, Toronto*

J. Robert Kellermann, *Lawyer, Toronto*

Gordon Kellett, *Journalist, Canim Lake BC*

Geoff Kelley, *Director of Communications, Alliance Quebec, Beaconsfield PQ*

Penn Kemp, *Writer, Flesherton ON*

Bill Kilbourn, *Writer, Toronto*

David Kilgour, *MP, Edmonton*

Anja Knickrehm, *Executive Secretary, Ottawa*

Jackie Koneak, *Vice-President, Kuujjuaq PQ*

Sheldon Korn, *Rabbi, Thornhill ON*

Meredith A. Kost, *Homemaker, Nepean ON*

Tom Kozar, *Instructor, Vancouver*

Sonya Kraemer, *Medical Secretary, Vancouver*

Robert Kroetsch, *Novelist, Victoria*

Judith Kucharsky, *Natl. Legal Counsel,Cdn.Inst.on Minority Rights*

Shalom Kurz, *Rabbi, London ON*

John Kuz, *Business Agent, Prince Rupert BC*

Angelo Lacalamita, *Retired*

Donald Lafreniere, *Campaign Coordinator, Winnipeg*

Christine Lalonde, *Illustrator, Montreal*

Ed Lam, *Race Relations Officer, Ottawa*

Ross Lambertson, *President, Canadian Rights & Liberties Federation*

Michele Landsberg, *Columnist, Toronto*

Eva Lapage, *Center Director, Kuujjuaq PQ*

Paul E. Lapage, *Field Worker, Kuujjuaq PQ*

Henriette Lapointe, *Ottawa*

Pierrette Lauzon, *Secretary, Vanier ON*

Harvey Larochelle, *Homemaker, Vancouver*

E.M. Lavalle, *College Instructor, Vancouver*

Donna Lavictoire, *Secretary, Orleans PQ*

Deidra Lawlor, *Orleans PQ*

Maria A. Leal, *Translator, Ottawa*

S. LeBlanc, *Director, Ottawa*

Lina Lebeau, *Lawyer, Kuujjuaq PQ*

Andrea Lebowitz, *University Lecturer, North Van. BC*

Mary Jo Leddy, *Journalist, Toronto*

Dennis Lee, *Writer, Toronto*

Fleur-Ange Lefebvre, *Professor, Ottawa*

Nicole Lefebvre, *Coordinator, Ottawa*

Mary Leftakis, *Student, Lasalle PQ*

Patricia Leibik, *Social Worker, Vancouver*

Diane Lemieux, *Student, Ottawa*

Louis M. Lenz, *Professor, Winnipeg*

E.D. Leppan, *Project Advisor, Ottawa*

P. Leroy, *Teacher, Montreal*

Bruce Leslie, *Editor, Toronto*

Douglas Leslie, *Journalist, Toronto*

Jean Leslie, *Retired, Montreal*
Rob Leslie, *Carpenter, Ottawa*
Andre Leveille, *Publisher, Montreal*
Maria Levesque, *Psycho-Education, Ottawa*
Michael A. Levine, *Lawyer, Toronto*
Alan Levitsky, *Student, St. Laurent PQ*
Felix Lion, *Retired Clergyman, Unitarian Church, Victoria*
George Little, *Postal Worker, Vancouver*
Don Longfield, *School Worker, Surrey BC*
Rowland Lorimer, *Professor, Burnaby BC*
Carolyn Luce, *Engineer, Ottawa*
Frances Lynn, *Educator, Vancouver*
Ken McBride, *Teacher, Trak BC*
Shauna McCabe, *Student, Orleans PQ*
Ileana McCaffrey, *Housewife, Ottawa*
G. MacCrimmon, *Teacher, Nepean ON*
Gregg Macdonald, *University Administrator, Fort Langley BC*
Donna L. MacDonald, *Writer, Nelson BC*
Jake MacDonald, *Writer, Winnipeg*
M. Angela MacDonald, *Social Worker, Ottawa*
Brian McDougall, *Student, Ottawa*
Alan MacFarlane, *Teacher, St. Laurent PQ*
Tom McGauley, *School Custodian, Burnaby*
Tom McGrath, *Teacher, St. Laurent PQ*
Paul McKane, *Optical Technician, Burnaby BC*
David S. MacKay, *Postal Worker, Vancouver*
Sharon E. McKay, *Writer, Brampton ON*
Bob MacKenzie, *Ont. MPP, Hamilton*
Barbara McKenzie, *Computer Operator, Nepean ON*
M. R. McKenzie, *Administrator, Ottawa*
John McLaren, *Law Professor, Victoria*
Murray McLauchlan, *Singer, Toronto*
Alice E. McLaughlin, *Housewife, Orleans PQ*
D. N. McLaughlin, *Member of Armed Forces, Orleans Charlene McLean, Clerk, Burnaby BC*
Margaret MacLean, *Professor, Ottawa*
Michael J. MacLean, *Professor, Ottawa*
N. Bruce McLeod, *Former Moderator, United Church of Canada*
Barclay F. H. McMillan, *Therapist, Ottawa*
Elsie McMurphy, *President, BC Teachers' Federation*
P.A. McRae, *Teacher, Ottawa*
Al Mackling, *Lawyer, Dugald MB*
Pat Mackling, *Homemaker, Dugald MB*
Holly N. Mackling, *Winnipeg*
Willie Makiuk, *Executive Assistant, Kuujjuaq PQ*
Lorne Mallin, *Assistant Newspaper Editor, Vancouver*
Maxine Malone, *Student, Ottawa*
Kim Maltman, *Physicist, Toronto*
Brenna L. Manders, *Research Assistant, Ottawa*
Cora-Lynne Mansell, *Student, Vancouver*
Dale Marcellus, *Millworker, Port Alberni BC*
Gilles Marchildon, *Student, Ottawa*
Frederick Margel, *Lawyer, Toronto*
Angela Marinos, *Student, Montreal*
Jimmy Mark, *Administrator, Kuujjuaq PQ*
David Marmorek, *Environmental Scientist, Vancouver*
Dow Marmur, *Rabbi, Toronto*
Michael Marrus, *Historian*

Dick Martin, *Union Officer*
Randall Martin, *Professor, West Vancouver BC*
Darlene Marzari, *BC MLA*
Bill Mason, *Filmmaker Old Chelsea PQ*
Hart Massey, *Retired Architect, Port Hope ON*
Melody Mastad, *Library Worker, Ottawa*
Jack Masters, *Mayor, Thunder Bay ON*
Roxanne E. Matheson, *Powell River BC*
G. Matrahazy, *Engineering Technologist, Ottawa*
Patricia Matson, *Graduate Student, Vancouver*
Gary Mauser, *Associate Professor, Coquitlam BC*

P. Lynn Mayer, *Researcher, Gloucester ON*
P. Maynard, *Chemist, Ottawa*
Linda Mead, *Administrator, Vancouver*
Virginia Medina, *Secretary, Gloucester ON*
Mary Meigs, *Painter, Westmount PQ*
Kim Meimar, *Student, Ottawa*
Joan Meister, *Disabled Rights Activist, Vancouver*
Louis Mercier, *Office Manager, Kuujjuaq PQ*
Hans Meyer, *Forester, Black Creek BC*
Mary Merrigan, *Nurse, Ottawa*
Christine Micklewright, *Union Officer, Vancouver*
J.S. Midanik, *Past President, Cdn. Civil Liberties Ass.*
Beverley Milligan, *Cook, Kamloops BC*
Beverley Mitchell, *Professor, Edmonton*
Margaret Mitchell, *MP, Vancouver East*
Rick Montemurro, *Operator, Langley BC*
Margaret Moore, *Bookseller, Renfrew ON*
Lisa Moores, *Mortgage Clerk, Coulds NF*
Lore Morcos, *Teacher, Ottawa*
Robert Morrow, *Mayor, Hamilton*
Khaled Mouammar, *Systems Analyst, Mississauga*
Edward C. Moulton, *Professor, Winnipeg*
Barbara Moyle, *Secretary, Vancouver*

Donna Munro, *Recreologist, Ottawa*
J.J. Munro, *President, Int'l. Woodworkers of America (Canada)*
Robert Munsch, *Children's Writer, Guelph ON*
Ellen Murray, *Lawyer, Toronto*
Jeanne Murray-Hicks, *Office Manager, Ottawa*
Lorraine Nadon, *Church Custodian, Ottawa*
Robert B. Nairne, *Union Rep, Oyama BC*
Winnie Napartuk, *Secretary, Kuujjuaq PQ*
Oli Narfason, *Farmer, Gimli MB*
V.R. Neufeld, *Physician, Hamilton*

B.E. Newell, *Government Employee, Ottawa*
Roxana Ng, *Professor, Fredericton*
bpNichol, *Poet, Toronto*
Jack Nichol, *President, United Fisherman & Allied Workers Union*
Irene Niechoda, *Graduate Student, Burnaby BC*
Fo Niemi, *Social Worker, Montreal*
Jeanne Norlin, *Licenced Practical Nurse, Burnaby BC*
Claire Northrop, *Retired, Sooke BC*
John Nunziata, *MP*
Susan O'Donnell, *Coordinator, BC Human Rights Coalition*
Stas Olpinski, *Biologist, Kuujjuaq PQ*
Michael Ondaatje, *Author, Toronto*
Zdenek Ondracek, *Consultant, Winnipeg*
Toni Onley, *Artist, Vancouver*
David Orlikow, *MP, Winnipeg North*
J. Gottfried Paasche, *Professor, Downsview ON*
Kaudjak Padlayat, *Receptionist, Kuujjuaq PQ*
S. Paine, *Nurse, Ottawa*
Andre Paradis, *Executive Director, Montreal*
Anothony Paré, *University Lecturer, Montreal*

Jory Parent, *Nurse, Nepean ON*
Erna Paris, *Historian*
Jean-Claude Parrot, *President, Canadian Union of Postal Workers*
Nicole Parton, *Journalist, Vancouver*
Ishvarhil Patel, *Student, Montreal*
Jordan Pearlson, *Rabbi, Toronto*
Michael G. Peers, *Primate, The Anglican Church of Canada*
M. Pelissier, *Nurse, Brockville ON*
Keith Penner, *MP, Cochrane-Superior*
Robert Penner, *Peace Activist, Toronto*
D. Peppard, *Dietary Aide, Castlegar BC*
Cecil Pereira, *Sociology Professor, Winnipeg*
Liette Perron, *Crises Intervention Worker, Ottawa*
Paul Peterson, *Alderman, New Denver BC*
C.I. Petros, *Teacher, Montreal*
Anita Phillips, *Nurse, Vancouver*
Rick Phillips, *Teacher, Don Mills ON*
Kathy Pickel, *Teacher, St. Laurent PQ*
Ruth Roach Pierson, *Historian, Toronto*
Suzanne Pilon, *Consultant, Cantley PQ*
Alison Pirot, *Writer, Regina*
Claudette Pitre, *Bank Teller, Vanier ON*
Gunther Plaut, *Rabbi, Toronto*
Roger Poirier, *Directeur General, Montreal*
Helen Porter, *Writer, St. John's*
James Porter, *Historian*
Rose Powell, *Housewife, Hamilton*
William Powell, *Retired Mayor of Hamilton*
Cyril Powles, *Professor, Toronto*
Allison Prentice, *Historian*
John Price, *Researcher, Vancouver*
J. Robert S. Prichard, *Law Professor, Toronto*
Russell Proux, *Photographer, Montreal*
Bordon Purcell, *Past Chairman, Ontario Human Rights Commission*
Betty-Anne Put, *Midwife, Arnprior ON*
Donna Quince, *Artistic Director, Ottawa*
Bob Rae, *MLA, Leader of the Official Opposition, ON*
B. Ragula, *President Byelorussian Canadian Co-ordinating Committee*
Chetan Rajani, *Writer, Ottawa*
Leyla Raphael, *President, World Conference on Religion and Peace, Canada*
Alan Redway, *MP, York East, ON*
Clyde Reed, *Professor, Burnaby BC*
Al Reford, *Vancouver*
Anne Reid, *Adminstrative Assistant, Ottawa*
Bill Reid, *Haida Artist, Vancouver*
Melissa Reid, *Student, Ottawa*
Roddy Reitmein, *Alderman, New Denver BC*
G. Rejskind, *Professor, Longueuil PQ*
Danielle Renaud, *Housewife, Ottawa*
Audrey Renault, *Community Legal Worker, Ottawa*
John Richards, *Professor, Burnaby BC*
Mordecai Richler, *Author, Montreal*
Dianna Rienstra, *Public Relations, Carleton Place ON*
Nelson Riis, *MP*
Shari Lynne Ritter, *Nurse, Nepean ON*
Catherine Robertson, *Kuujjuaq PQ*
Svend Robinson, *MP*

> *"Canadians of every background are supporting the National Association of Japanese Canadians' demand for redress as a necessary journey into the interior of our national conscience. Acknowledgement of an imperfect past is a prerequisite for a future in which people live together in mutual respect, and self-righteous racism does not take us by surprise again."*
>
> Bruce McLeod, *former Moderator of the United Church of Canada, in his column, "Mulroney Is Failing Japanese Canadians," Toronto Star, April 19, 1988.*

Kevin Roch, *Clerk, St. Rose PQ*

Bruce Rogers, *Broadcaster*

R. Roman, *Professor*

Alan Rose, *Executive Vice-President, Canadian Jewish Congress*

Jeff Rose, *Pres., Canadian Union of Public Emp.*

Teya Rosenberg, *Student, Ottawa*

Philip Rosensweig, *Rabbi, Kitchener ON*

Michael Ross, *Teacher, Elkford BC*

Marilyn Rossner, *Professor, St. Laurent PQ*

Abraham Rotstein, *Professor, Toronto*

Alex Rougeau, *Groundman, Coquitlam BC*

David Roy, *Student, Vancouver*

Clayton C. Ruby, *Lawyer, Toronto*

Stuart Rush, *Lawyer, Vancouver*

Stanley Ryerson, *Historian*

C. Sabourin, *Counsellor, Ottawa*

Lucinda St. George, *Student, Ottawa*

Keith A.P. Sandiford, *Professor, Winnipeg*

Jyoti Sanghera, *Human Rights Activist, New Westminster BC*

Mae Saunders, *Receptionist, Kuujjuaq PQ*

Janet Sawyer, *Clerical Worker, Vancouver*

Richard Savaria, *Plumber, Kuujjuaq PQ*

Ebrahim Sayed, *Occupational Therapist, Fonthill ON*

Audrey Schirmer, *Teacher, Montreal*

Edward Scott, *Archibishop, Anglican Church of Canada*

Joan Selby, *Researcher, Ottawa*

Deborah L. Sereacki, *Clerk, Winnipeg*

Sybil Shack, *Pres., Cdn. Civil Liberties Assoc.(Man.)*

Hari Sharma, *Associate Professor, Vancouver*

Roisin Sheehy-Culhane, *Office Administrator, Burnaby BC*

David Sheldon, *Librarian, Port Moody BC*

Brian Shenker, *Student, Montreal*

Charlie Shipaluk, *Supervisor, Kuujjuaq PQ*

Israel N. Silverman, *Rabbi, Hamilton*

Carolyn Sinclair, *Women's Shelter Worker, Ottawa*

Donald W. Sjoberg, *Bishop, Evangelical Lutheran Churches*

Eileen May Skillen, *Instructor, Scarborough ON*

Reuben Slonim, *Rabbi, Toronto*

Carol Lee Smith, *Student, Toronto*

Claire Smith, *Translator, Kuujjuaq PQ*

Eileen Smith, *Library Clerk, Burnaby BC*

Nancy Smith, *Statistician, Ottawa*

Mendy Solak, *Administrator, Montreal*

Hans Speich, *Manager, Montreal*

Doug Sprague, *Professor, Winnipeg*

Anne Squire, *Moderator, United Church of Canada*

Alanna Stalker Horner, *Teacher, Montreal*

John Stanton, *Retired Lawyer, Vancouver*

Jo-Anne Stasiuk, *Chaplain, Ottawa*

Harold Steeves, *Alderman, Richmond BC*

Lionel Steiman, *Professor, Winnipeg*

C. Stephen, *Self-Employed, Nepean ON*

Homer Stevens, *Delta BC*

Diane Stewart, *Photocopier, Ottawa*

Richard E. Stone, *Engineer, Ottawa*

James J. Strachan, *Hospital Chaplain, Ottawa*

George C. Stratton, *Retired, Belleville ON*

Lydia Jean Stratton, *Cashier, Belleville ON*

Howard Stutt, *Professor, Montreal*

Milo F. Suchma, *Pres., Czechoslovak Association of Canada*

Carl B. Sullivan, *Technician, Edmonton*

Wayne Sumner, *Professor*

Wilbur Sutherland, *President, Imago*

Hilary Syme, *Consultant, Ottawa*

Ruth Syme, *Presbyterian Minister, Toronto*

L. Szkambara, *Student, Ottawa*

Lucia Szkwarek, *Winnipeg*

Ludwik Szkwarek, *Diesel Mechanic, Winnipeg*

Lada Tamarack, *Social Worker, Ottawa*

Larisa Tarwick, *College Teacher, Terrace BC*

Catherine Taylor, *Insurance Agent, Vancouver*

P. Tennenhouse, *Civil Servant, Ottawa*

Donna Thomas, *Custodian, Gibsons BC*

Paul G. Thomas, *Professor, Winnipeg*

Elijah Thomassiah, *TV Producer, Salluit PQ*

Elizabeth Thompson, *Student, Ottawa*

John H. Thompson, *Historian, Montreal*

Kathryn Thornton, *Minister, Greenfield Park PQ*

Carole Tillman, *Research Assistant, Ottawa*

Jo Tombaugh, *Professor, Ottawa*

Charlie Tooma, *Production Assistant, Kuujjuaq PQ*

Sandy Tooma, *Announcer, Kuujjuaq PQ*

Frances Trant, *Employment Equity Co-ordinator, Ottawa*

Helene Tremblay, *Fonctionnaire, Hull PQ*

Camylle Tremblay-Choquette, *Coordinator, Vanier*

Rhea Tregebov, *Writer, Toronto*

Pat Trites, *Nurse, Orleans PQ*

Lawrence Troster, *Rabbi, Richmond Hill ON*

Denise Tsakalaki, *Student, PQ*

J.L.D. Turnbull, *Millworker, Gibsons BC*

Hanny Turner-Pannekoek, *Social Worker, Victoria*

T.E. Vadney, *Professor, Winnipeg*

Marc Van Ameringer, *Economist, Ottawa*

E.P. van Beek, *Editor, Ottawa*

Gerald Vandezande, *Public Affairs Director, Agincourt ON*

Evelina Vaupotic, *Cook, Richmond BC*

Ray Viand, *Bookstore Manager, Vancouver*

Gregory Volk, *Custodian, Toronto*

Duc Hoa Vuong, *Underwriter, Victoria*

Ian Waddell, *MP*

Paul Wadden, *Carpenter, Vancouver*

Sean Wadelius, *Correctional Officer, The Pas MB*

Vaughan Wadelius, *Teacher, The Pas MB*

Evelyn S. Wajcer, *Professor, Westmount PQ*

Doug Waldron, *Computer Analyst, Winnipeg*

G.M. Walker, *Dept. of National Defence, Gloucester*

Megan Wardrop, *Educator, Ottawa*

Wayne Waters, *Geologist, Vancouver*

Patrick Watson, *Broadcaster, Toronto*

Eric Waugh, *Ships Rigger, Vancouver*

Anne Webb, *Sales Executive, Ashton ON*

Phyllis Webb, *Writer, Ganges BC*

Rudy Weibe, *Writer, Edmonton*

Kathleen Weil, *Lawyer, Montreal*

Merrily Weisbord, *Broadcaster, Montreal*

Elliot Weisgarber, *Retired Professor, Vancouver*

Kathleen Whipp, *Counsellor, Ottawa*

Reg Whitaker, *Professor*

Anna Mae White, *Student*

Arthur A. White, *Retired, Honey Harbour ON*

Heather White, *Counsellor, Ottawa*

Bill Whitehead, *Cannington ON*

Paul & Joan Whitney, *Librarians, Vancouver*

Elaine Whittaker, *Administrative Assistant, Ottawa*

Joyce Wieland, *Artist, Toronto*

Jill Wight, *Teacher, Port Moody BC*

M. Wileman, *Postal Worker, Vancouver*

Bob Williams, *MLA, BC*

Susan Williams, *Secretary, Ottawa*

Dorothy Wills, *Teacher, Anjou PQ*

F. Wilson, *Organizer, Vancouver*

Gordon Wilson, *Pres., Ontario Federation of Labour*

Lois Wilson, *President, World Council of Churches*

Mary Anne Wilson, *Consultant, Ottawa*

Karen Woo, *Student, Montreal*

R. H. Wood, *Retired, Vanier ON*

A. Wright, *Health Planner, Ottawa*

Allan Young, *Retired Railroad Worker, North Burnaby*

David Young, *Writer, Toronto*

Diana Young, *Teacher, Kanata ON*

Frank Young, *Public Servant, Kanata ON*

Joan Young, *Law Student, Victoria*

Neil Young, *MP, Beaches, ON*

Jozef Zabawa, *Carpenter, Winnipeg*

G. Zador, *Program Officer, Chelsea PQ*

Bill Zander, *Carpenter, New Westminster BC*

Frederick Zemans, *Law Professor*

ORGANIZATIONS

Affiliation of Multicultural Societies and Service Agencies of BC

Alberta Association of Social Workers

The Anglican Church of Canada

Association of United Ukrainian Canadians, Branch 64, Vernon

BC Association of Social Workers

BC Federation of Labour

BC Human Rights Coalition

BC Organization to Fight Racism

BC Teachers' Federation Program Against Racism

Byelorussian Canadian Co-ordinating Committee

Canadian Arab Federation

Canadian Auto Workers, Local 2171

Canadian Baptist Federation

Canadian Civil Liberties Association (Manitoba)

Canadian Council of Catholic Bishops, Human Rights Committee

Canadian Council of Christians & Jews (Alberta)

Canadian Federation of Multicultural Councils

Canadian Hispanic Congress

Canadian Hungarian Society of Victoria, BC

Canadian Institute on Minority Rights, Montreal

Canadian Lithuanian Community

Canadian Rights and Liberties Federation

Canadian Union of Postal Workers

Canadian Union of Public Employees, Loc. 394

Chinese Benevolent Association of Canada

Chinese Canadian National Council

Committee for Racial Justice

Communist Party of Canada

Council of Muslim Communities of Canada

Federation of Sikh Societies of Canada

First Portugese Canadian Club

German Canadian Congress

Greenwood Board of Trade

Hellenic Canadian Congress

Humanist Association of Greater Vancouver

Independent Pictures Inc.

Indian People's Association in North America

Inter-Cultural Association of Greater Victoria

International Woodworkers of America - Canada

Korean Canadian Cultural Assocation of Metropolitan Toronto

Latin-American Action Research Centre

Latvian National Federation in Canada

Manitoba Intercultural Council

Multicultural Council of Saskatchewan

National Council of Jamaicans and Supportive Organizations in Canada

National Farmers Union

Okanagan Women's Coalition

Pacific Immigrant Resources Society

Press Gang Printers & Publishers

Prince Rupert Amalgamated Shoreworkers & Clerks Union

Prisoners' Rights Group

Public Service Alliance of Canada

Richmond Multicultural Concerns Society

Students & Teachers Opposing Prejudice, Red Deer

Surrey Delta Immigrant Services Society

United Church of Canada

United Council of Filipino Associations in Canada

United Fishermen and Allied Workers Union

Vancouver Island Human Rights Coalition

Writers' Union of Canada

York University Faculty Association

Ottawa Redress Rally,
April 14, 1988

(right) **Hide (Hyodo) Shimizu, giving a toast at the banquet the evening before the rally.** *Photo: Gordon King.*

(left) **Rick Shiomi, member of the taiko group "Wasabi Daiko," performing at the banquet the evening before the rally.** *Photo: Gordon King.*

(above) **Japanese Canadians chartered two buses from Toronto. Getting off the bus are Ken Kishibe, editor of the** Nikkei Voice, **and Shirley Yamada.**
Photo: Gordon King.

(above) **Beginning the march, Fred Kagawa, World War II veteran, from Toronto.** *Photo: Gordon King.*

118

(above) **Marching towards the Parliament Buildings. At the front of the line, from left to right: Mary Obata and Roger Obata, NAJC Vice-President, from Toronto; Mas Kawanami, from Calgary; Bill Kobayashi, President, NAJC Toronto Chapter; George Kadota, from** Toronto; Kyoshi Shimizu, from Victoria; Charles Kadota, from Vancouver. *Photo: Gordon King.*

(below) **David Suzuki, Art Miki, and Mary Jo Leddy.** *Photo: Gordon King.*

(above) **Terry Watada, singing at the opening of the Forum.** *Photo: Gordon King.*

119

(above) **David Suzuki signing his autograph for a fan.**
Photo: John Flanders.

(right)
Shirley Yamada, from Toronto.
Photo: John Flanders.

(above right and right)
At the Redress Forum.
Photo: Gordon King.

Can it Happen Again?

The NAJC Redress Proposal included a recommendation that the War Measures Act be amended to ensure that similar injustices not recur in the future, and that the government make a serious commitment to review and amend the Charter of Rights and Freedoms to guarantee that the rights of individuals cannot ever again be abrogated on the basis of ancestry.

On July 21, 1988, just two months before the redress settlement, the War Measures Act was abolished, and replaced by the Emergencies Act. Although the new legislation is not perfect, it is much better than the government's original draft, because of the efforts of the NAJC Legal Affairs Committee.

Co-chair of the NAJC's Legal Affairs Committee, Ann Sunahara, drafted a 65-page submission for presentation to the Parliamentary Legislative Committee considering the Bill. At first, to speed up the committee process, the Committee was not going to hear submissions from ethnic groups but the NAJC argued that Japanese Canadians had a special interest in this issue.

The NAJC submission to the Committee in March 1988 showed that the injustices of the past could be repeated under the new Act as it was first drafted. As in the 1940s, Parliament would not be able to halt the abuse of power, and the proposed compensation provisions were subject to political will because they would be controlled by the very government that had invoked the emergency powers under this new Act.

As a result of the NAJC submission, the NDP Committee members and the government both proposed numerous amendments that reflected the NAJC's concerns. The revisions included:

- restrictions on when the emergency powers could be used;
- expansion of Parliament's ability to supervise the Cabinet's use of the emergency powers;
- power to Parliament to revoke an order in council;
- provision of a mandatory inquiry into the use of emergency power;
- mandatory compensation for abuse of emergency power;
- a ban on "the detention, imprisonment or internment of Canadian Citizens or landed immigrants...on the basis of race, national or ethnic origin, colour, religion, sex, age or mental or physical disability."

As Ann Sunahara has said, "The new Emergencies Act is a great improvement over the War Measures Act, but perhaps its greatest flaw is that it is only an Act of Parliament. It can be abolished at any time and replaced with something worse" ("The Emergencies Act: A Gift to Canadians," *Nikkei Voice*, November 1989). The only way to absolutely ensure that the history of Japanese Canadians will not be repeated is to amend the Charter of Rights and Freedoms to ensure that human rights can never be eroded, even in time of emergency.

121

The marchers left placards and ribbons around the Peace Flame.

Photo: Gordon King.

"*I think of the word 'justice.' Too many people in this world have a concept of justice as one thing: 'Just us.' We can't just look at ourselves and say justice will come by itself. It never will.*"

George Watts, Nuu-chah-nulth Tribal Council, at a Redress Rally in Vancouver, March 1988; quoted in "This Week's Question," The West Ender, Vancouver, March 17, 1988.

On April 14, 1988, busloads of senior Japanese Canadians from Montreal, Hamilton and Toronto converged on Parliament Hill, and were joined there by other Japanese Canadians from all across Canada who arrived by plane. An estimated 500, the vast majority of whom were victims of internment, had come to call on the government to finally resolve the redress issue through a negotiated settlement with the NAJC. Some carried placards with slogans, others carried "Ribbons of Hope," containing names of Japanese Canadians who had not been able to attend but who had donated so that others could be there. As they marched past the House of Commons they chanted "Redress Now," making their way to the Confederation Room in the West Block of the Parliament Buildings, where the Redress Forum took place.

As the speeches began, it became clear that Japanese Canadians were no longer alone in their struggle for justice. The National Coalition for Japanese Canadian Redress reflected the conscience of Canadians who had come to realize the importance of redress as a major human rights issue—and one that had to be resolved through direct negotiations with the Japanese Canadians whose rights had been violated in the 1940s. The speakers represented a wide spectrum of ethnic communities, politicians, civil rights organizations, and religious associations who supported the NAJC.

Surprisingly, the newly-appointed Minister of State for Multiculturalism, Gerry Weiner, attended to make his first statement on the issue. But the anticipation which had animated the crowd quickly dissipated, as his speech appeared simply to justify the old offers. For forty years governments had refused to acknowledge, much less redress the injustices, he said, and that insensitivity had carried through to Pierre Trudeau. He reviewed Crombie's

Photo: John Flanders.

123

offer of an acknowledgment, legislative changes, and a $12 million community fund, but did not address the issue of what would be fair compensation. His reference to the Prime Minister's deep feelings for human rights seemed empty, given that the NAJC had not been able to meet with the Prime Minister in three and a half years.

The only seed of hope he offered was his willingness to reopen talks with the NAJC—a gesture that seemed, at the time, nothing more than a political formality so that his party could say they were "in discussions" when the next election was called.

In front of the speakers' podium lay piles of campaign postcards with some 15,000 signatures of Canadians in support of the NAJC's call for a negotiated settlement on them. Immediately after the rally speeches, these postcards were hand delivered to the Prime Minister's office by three formerly interned Japanese Canadians.

The Ottawa Rally was the high point in the NAJC's campaign. Since Japanese Canadians had never before congregated so dramatically in Ottawa to challenge the government's failure to settle redress in a just and honourable manner, the event received powerful media coverage. Senior Canadian citizens, the victims of the injustices, were enacting their democratic right to demand "justice in our time," the title of the pamphlet distributed by the NAJC for the occasion.

In his opening speech, NAJC President Art Miki stressed the urgency of the redress issue in the Japanese Canadian community. Many seniors who were directly affected by the wartime injustices were passing away without seeing the issue resolved, despite the popular support for redress by Canadians.

"...We have many postcards right in front of us signed by Canadians from all walks of life who are interested in this justice issue, this human rights issue, and are saying let's get it resolved, let's not let it go by any longer. For four or five years we've been pressing to get people to recognize that the history of our community needs to be told. Through gatherings such as this, and rallies and forums across the country, we're trying to educate Canadians that there's a lesson to be learned for the future of our country in what happened to Japanese Canadians."

In the speeches that followed were strong and moving statements endorsing the NAJC's struggle for justice.

LEWIS CHAN,
TREASURER, CANADIAN ETHNOCULTURAL COUNCIL

The Canadian Ethnocultural Council has thirty-six member national ethnic associations. On the CEC's resolution to support the NAJC's position on individual compensation:

> "Given that certain communities have faced injustices in Canada in the past, be it resolved that the Canadian Ethnocultural Council Redress Committee continue to work regarding past injustices against various communities. Be it further resolved that the Canadian Ethnocultural Council call on the federal government to undertake immediate negotiations with the National Association of Japanese Canadians to seek compensation and apology agreement acceptable to the National Association of Japanese Canadians.
>
> "Further, in October of 1987, there was a unanimous resolution passed by our Board of National Presidents which called for a settlement which would include individual compensation."

Archbishop Ted Scott
Photo: Gordon King.

Archbishop Ted Scott,
Anglican Church of Canada

On his memory of the uprooting of Japanese Canadians:

"I remember children going home from school with their books, crying because they'd been told they had to be taken away, and leave. The children crying were both of Japanese origin, Canadians, and white people, friends who had been in school together. I remember going to the Matsumoto Boat Works in Prince Rupert and talking to the people working there. Then later I remember going to Hastings Park and spending two or three days with the people in Hastings Park where they were interned. I remember scenes of Japanese fishing boats brought in without any time for people to make adequate arrangements to store them, and tied up alongside, and gradually vandalized, and many of them almost totally destroyed. I remember all that, and remember also meetings with the RCMP who said that this move was not necessary. There was no real danger from this community.

And I remember the way in which, under the pressure of the war attitude, emotions were kindled in Vancouver, and individual people giving leadership to kindling those emotions, that led to the decision finally under the pressure of that situation to intern and remove. Later, as the Bishop of the Kootenay, I visited communities in Slocan, Greenwood and New Denver where internment camps had been set up, and met with some of the people who still remained in those areas. So I'm not talking about something abstract. I am talking about human relationships and people, and I am talking about justice."

Ernie Epp
Photo: John Flanders.

Ernie Epp,
Multiculturalism Critic, the New Democratic Party

On the need for a negotiated redress settlement:

"The issue of redress for Japanese Canadian losses, dispossession, uprooting suffered during the Second World War is the most burning issue amongst the ethnocultural communities facing the Canadian government.

"...I regret enormously with you that governments past have failed to deal with it and I regret that we're still waiting in the early months of 1988 for action. Amongst the specific activities that I have been able to undertake on behalf of the cause of redress is working to ensure in January of 1985 that no arbitrary action was taken by the government at the time which did not have the support of all the parties in the House of Commons. And it appeared briefly, after the negotiations promised in December of 1984 were broken off by the government, that there might be a resolution proposed. I have said in other places, and repeat here the categorical observation, that it seems inconceivable to me that a great injustice done by arbitrary action of a government during the 1940s, and maintained by arbitrary actions, could ever be redressed by arbitrary action now. We feel that very deeply, and for that reason, we are convinced that redress must be negotiated. We can play around with the word Mr. Minister [addressing Gerry Weiner], but whether it's closed discussions or whatever, respect for a community requires negotiations to arrive at a redress acceptable to the community."

Announcing the NDP's support for individual compensation:

"I want to say here on behalf of my leader, the Honourable Ed Broadbent, and the New Democratic caucus that we are committed to individual compensation. If we had the opportunity, thanks to the decisions of the Canadian people, to form a government we would establish an arbitration process to achieve that compensation. We would look to precedents in other countries where compensation has been awarded to individuals, we would consider carefully the case that has been made by the National Association of Japanese Canadians, and we would arrive at a figure for individual compensation."

On the NAJC's role in the hearings on the new Emergencies Act to replace the War Measures Act:

"...I say that to the credit of the Honourable Perrin Beatty, Minister of National Defence, that he was prepared to accept large improvements in the Bill [replacing the War Measures Act]. Late yesterday the government added a clause which will prohibit, once the Bill has become law, any internment of civilians on the basis of race. And my colleague suggested that was to your [the NAJC's] credit for having made the case so forcefully and for coming here to Ottawa to underscore it. So thank you on behalf of all the peoples of Canada for what you are doing to make this a better country—to make it the kind of Canada we want it to be."

GILLES TARDIF,
CANADIAN FEDERATION OF RIGHTS AND FREEDOMS

On redress as a justice issue [translated from the French]:

"In this fortieth anniversary of the Universal Declaration of Human Rights, it is important that Canada, in revising its emergency legislation and the War Measures Act, rely on the lessons drawn from the last World War, and that it put an end to measures in which arbitrary actions and discriminatory attacks on fundamental rights unfortunately were made acts of law.

"It is for this reason that the Canadian Federation has joined with the National Coalition for Japanese Canadian Redress to demand justice, to demand of the Canadian government, represented here by Mr. Weiner, that it abide by its own principles and that it enter negotiations without delay, because it seems to us that we should take this opportunity to plant the seeds for a future in which we give rights and freedoms the greatest importance in our lives.

"In conclusion, I would just like to say that we must not believe that by limiting the issue posed by Japanese Canadians to simply a multiculturalism portfolio, we avoid the problem of justice, because this injustice done to Canadians of Japanese origin was done to each individual among them, it was done to the whole community, and it has affected all Canadians. All of us present here together with the organizations in the coalition are going to demand that the Canadian government take advantage of this special year to make some concrete gestures and to obtain justice for Canadians of Japanese origin."

ALAN BOROVOY,
CANADIAN CIVIL LIBERTIES ASSOCIATION

On the importance of redress for the future protection of rights:

"Japanese Canadians have been criticized for this campaign. You're told to 'put the past behind you. Live in the present. What about all the other injustices in our society? Don't be so provincial. Don't be so self-obsessed'.

"By your campaign of seeking compensation, you are not living in the past, you are working for the future. You are helping to create a precedent from which future governments would find it very hard to retreat. You're serving notice to whoever is

Alan Borovoy
Photo: Gordon King.

going to be in government, that from now to the end of time, to whatever extent they are tempted, to depart so radically from the norms of civilized behaviour, at the very least there will be a price to pay. And it is in that sense the decisions made about Japanese Canadians will create an obstacle and a deterrent against abuse of other people—of Blacks, of Native people, of Pakistanis, of East Indians, of refugees, and of all the vulnerable people whom I hope we will be welcoming to this country. This campaign is not parochialism by Japanese Canadians—it is social justice for everybody. You are fighting not only for you but also for us. Instead of our criticisms, you deserve our commendations."

SISTER MARY JO LEDDY,
ROMAN CATHOLIC CHURCH

On the value of redress:

"There are those who will quibble about the cost of redress for Japanese Canadians. I would say simply that this is the best investment we can make

Sister Mary Jo Leddy
Photo: John Flanders.

in the future of this country—in ensuring democracy and justice in this country; in ensuring that this kind of thing will never happen again for anyone. That is a far better investment in democracy than one more submarine in the North. As Archbishop Scott said so well, no matter what the amount it really can never recompense for what people lost. We cannot make the past better. But we can make the future better for all of us. Redress for Japanese Canadians is part of our commitment together to a country which has a just and a hopeful future."

SERGIO MARCHI,
MULTICULTURALISM CRITIC, THE LIBERAL PARTY

On the impact of the rally:

"...I think today in this room we are collectively sharing that pain and that agony in front of our country. And that agony was created by a mistake of a government. And I learned very early on, as we all do, that we must learn from our mistakes, and yet it saddens me that successive governments

Sergio Marchi *Photo: Gordon King.*

have not been able to learn the teaching that is passed on to all of us when we are youngsters. A government of the past turned back a boat of Jewish refugees, the Saint Louis, and yet in 1988 we have a government that wants to push forward a law to give it the opportunity of turning back future boats of refugees. We had a government during wartime that interned Japanese Canadians and we live in 1988 with governments who fail to acknowledge that mistake. I don't profess and I don't pretend, as a member of the Liberal Party, to come here with very clean hands. Yet I am prepared to say that never has there been a window of opportunity like there has been in the past almost four years because of the heightened sensitivity and awareness by the Canadian public to this issue; and rather than take advantage of that window of opportunity we have wasted to date that opportunity collectively."

On redress as a justice issue:

"It is not purely a multicultural issue. It is not an ethnic issue. It is an issue of injustice against Canadian citizens in Canada, in their own land...and therefore the Justice Minister of this country, where it first began, ought to have been

David Suzuki *Photo: Gordon King.*

Class at Pine Crescent School, during the internment at Slocan City. Seated on far right is author Joy Kogawa, and in back row, far left, is broadcaster and scientist David Suzuki. *Courtesy of Tom Oikawa.*

the lead minister so that very clearly and very early on we would not confuse the issue or fuel the perception in the country that somehow this is an ethnic thing, that this is a multicultural thing and that some people 'want something' again."

On the importance of process:

"[We should] have a real process that gives justice an opportunity to become realized, and not only a series of unconnected meetings to discuss generalities only, to have two solitudes digging in the trenches and this great vacuum in between without a bridge. And therefore, while we need to talk about substance, and compensation, and acknowledgements, and how we prevent the situation from happening again, I encourage you to take the message to the government today that in addition to requesting their attention on the substance that you demand a commitment to an honourable and effective process, a mechanism that would overcome these shortcomings and offer the hope of reaching a just settlement. And I

regret to say, and I'm being honest with you, that unless we have this process, this atmosphere of give and take, and a sense of compromise which has been a Canadian landmark in many situations in this country, I remain skeptical that a fair and honourable solution can be reached. And therefore I request of the new Minister of State for Multiculturalism, the Honourable Gerry Weiner, to show some strength and some courage and to provide, for the very first time in his government and in previous governments, a process that will realistically and honestly give justice a chance to succeed."

DAVID SUZUKI,

BROADCASTER AND SCIENTIST.

On the impact of the redress movement:

"I was honoured when I was asked to appear here, and I feel absolutely elated to see the many friends of Japanese Canadians who are now supporting the issues that we're concerned with. As I sat here I remembered the day, twenty years ago this month, when Martin Luther King was assassinated. Two days after the assassination the University of British Columbia asked me to speak at a rally in his memory. At that time I pointed out that his death should not be allowed to simply go by way of our memory and disappear, but that what he symbolized was someone who was battling for issues that concerned us very much, including the Japanese Canadian issue, the injustice that had been done to us. And the next day the Vancouver *Sun* wrote an editorial chastising me and saying that, after all, war is war, and conditions were different then, and saying that people shouldn't be raising old memories like that. We should let them go and forget about them. And I think it's to Art's and many other people's credit that they have continued to press the issue of redress and the Vancouver *Sun* wouldn't dare publish an editorial like that today—and you must take a lot of credit for that.

"My mother was born in Vancouver, raised and lived her entire life in Canada, never went to Japan in her whole life, although I urged her to many times. She died at the age of 74 and I bitterly resent that she died without ever having known an official apology for not having been an enemy of this country. My father will be 80 in January next year. He's already had two operations for cancer. I hope he'll go to 100—I know he won't. And I see many people sitting here—I wish you could go on for another twenty years as well. But you won't. And I urge you, Mr. Weiner, in your new position, to look at these people and to do everything you can; urge your government to enter into a serious negotiation and for once end a lot of the great hurt—and the injustice that should have been settled long ago."

On the role of Japanese Canadians in the larger struggle for human rights:

"...A country is not defined by all of the wonderful words written down in its Constitution, or the magnificent speeches given by its leaders. Nor is it defined by what it is when times are good. What defines a country is what we do—our actions—in times of stress. Those are the times when these great ideas of freedom, of equality, and justice matter. That's why we go to war and die. Because we must guarantee those in times of stress. We failed miserably as a country to live up to those words and ideas in 1942, and tragically we didn't learn from that and we flunked miserably again in October 1970. The role that Japanese Canadians play in Canada is to be living reminders of our failure as a country to live up to these ideas. Not to make people feel guilty, but to remind people of how fragile democracy is. Just as Jews do not let us forget the Holocaust to prevent its recurrence, so Japanese Canadians must serve a role of never letting Canadians forget the injustice perpetrated against Canadians of Japanese origin.

"...I see the current demand for an official apology and for some kind of settlement, not only as an issue of justice. It gives us the opportunity to educate Canadians by reminding them of the past. And every time I get letters or phone calls, and I get many, from people who say, 'How dare you ask for redress after what you did to us, to our soldiers in Hong Kong or Southeast Asia,' I am glad because we've brought another bigot out into the open.

"...As victims of a great injustice, I also believe that Japanese Canadians assume an extra burden. We, the victims, know from experience the effects of racism and bigotry. And so ours must be the first voices raised whenever we see prejudice rear up. Whether it's bigotry extended towards Blacks,

Sikhs, Jews, boat people, homosexuals, or women, Japanese Canadians must be at the forefront of the fight against it. That is our burden. And so, I conclude by reiterating again, Mr. Weiner, you and your party stand at a very opportune moment to settle this issue, and I feel very hopeful that something will be done before the next election.

"But we will not stop there. I urge all of you, my brothers and sisters from the Japanese Canadian community, to broaden your vision and the force of your concerns to include the greatest victims in our society today. I'm speaking, of course, of the aboriginal peoples of Canada. They have pledged their support for our efforts and I'm very moved and humbled by that. Because the past and continued treatment of the original inhabitants of this country is nothing short of barbaric. We cannot speak of Canada as a just place, a democracy, a country of equality for all, so long as we fail to address native claims and native rights. And so I urge all of you to look on our struggle for justice for the Japanese Canadian community as just the beginning of a much greater struggle."

GERRY WEINER,
MINISTER OF STATE FOR MULTICULTURALISM

On his intention to reopen talks with the NAJC:

"Last year my predecessor, Mr. Crombie, promised an official government acknowledgement of the injustice to be adopted formally by Parliament, the introduction of new emergency legislation to replace the War Measures Act, and $12 million for a Japanese Canadian community fund. Sadly, it proved impossible to come to a mutually satisfactory agreement as to what would be fair and responsible financially. And so here we are today,

not in anger, on either side, but with genuine regret that we have not yet fully come together. I want to compliment you for your dedication to seeing justice done and for organizing this important rally here to highlight the importance of this issue for Canadians. This is my second week as Minister of State for Multiculturalism. It is with great interest that I look forward to meeting with you, listening to what you have to say and exploring the full complexity of this issue. My door is open to you because the government continues to be at one with you in our determination to see this matter dealt with in a fair and timely manner. We all know today that there was no justification in military or security necessity for the wartime relocations, internments, and property seizures. We all know today that the extent of postwar deportations and deprivations of civil rights was utterly shameful. We all understand today that this blot on the reputation and character of Canada has to be recognized formally and appropriate redress made."

Gerry Weiner
Photo: Gordon King.

ROY MIKI,

CHAIRPERSON, GREATER VANCOUVER JAPANESE CANADIAN CITIZENS' ASSOCIATION REDRESS COMMITTEE

On the growing strength of the redress movement:

"The level of articulation, the level of comprehension, the level of awareness and the level of compassion that I heard in the words of the speakers, was music to my ears—music because five years ago we would be speaking in various places and we would encounter, over and over again, massive ignorance about our community's history and experiences. The redress movement has turned all that around, and the speeches here today bring this powerfully home."

On the silence of the past:

"I think it was the community's own burden that led to a silence throughout the 1950s and the 1960s. There was the desire to put a painful experience behind, but also the fact that the homes, the properties, the community facilities, the place in BC that had been 'Japanese Canadian' was gone. There was no point in dwelling on the past, but only the very important question of survival in the present. During the 1970s, some of us were very lucky to be a part of a reawakening and a rethinking. Then we, as a community, were finally able to gain access to the government's own documents and files, and there we were told in black and white print by Ministers and policy advisors of the government of the day, that what was being done to Japanese Canadians was unnecessary and an abrogation of citizenship rights—that it was done as a political measure."

On the struggle to undertake political action to seek redress:

"The government's dispersal policy in 1945 said to Japanese Canadians, and I paraphrase Prime Minister Mackenzie King, 'We will distribute your numbers equally across Canada so that you will no longer cause racial hatred.' The victims of racism were punished and those who perpetuated the racism were let alone. As a result of dispersal our communities were redistributed all across Canada. But when we began the redress movement, one of the first criticisms of our government, and I paraphrase the first Minister who said, 'Get your act together. You people are not unanimous. I can find people who disagree with the NAJC in Toronto. There are others who disagree with you elsewhere.' And I remember saying, 'Mr. Minister, are you aware that your government instituted a policy which was meant to destroy the community, and that the policy worked. Our community is no longer unified but we are struggling across thousands of miles and lives that have been lived apart—we are trying politically to reassemble and to reunify, and this is a major force in our history at this time.'"

THE
FINAL PHASE

KAWABATA
00672

NEGOTIATIONS WITH GERRY WEINER

(below) **Lucien Bouchard, Secretary of State, with Rick Clippendale, opening negotiations at the Ritz-Carlton Hotel in Montreal, August 24, 1988.**
Photo: Cassandra Kobayashi.

(above) **Roy Miki and Art Miki.** Photo: Cassandra Kobayashi.

On June 15, 1988, members of the NAJC Strategy Committee first met with Gerry Weiner, Chief of Staff Dennison Moore, and advisor Rick Clippendale in Winnipeg. The language of this meeting was different from that of previous meetings with the government. Weiner's approach reflected a change in attitudes; he reported that the Prime Minister now wanted to explore all aspects of the redress question, beginning with the NAJC's position. The issue of individual compensation would be considered, but how would a figure be determined? Would a government commission or committee be acceptable? The NAJC, aware that the US redress bill might soon be signed into law by President Ronald Reagan, responded by saying that the settlement had to be comparable to the American bill and that individual compensation would have to be included. The meeting concluded with an agreement to meet in early July to discuss a process.

The July meeting did not occur as planned, and as the days dragged on without a commitment from Weiner, the NAJC began to lose confidence. Perhaps, yet again, the government was stalling—until the anticipated elections in the fall.

Meanwhile, on August 4, 1988, US President Ronald Reagan announced his acceptance of the American redress Bill HR442, and in a letter to the Speaker of the House of Representatives, stated:

> The enactment of HR442 will close a sad chapter in American history in a way that reaffirms America's commitment to the preservation of liberty and justice for all.

On August 10, 1988, the President signed HR442 into law.

Pressure in the House of Commons heated up following the American settlement, as Multicultural Critics Sergio Marchi and Ernie Epp challenged Prime Minister Mulroney to keep his 1984 promise to compensate Japanese Canadians. Mulroney responded:

> There are ongoing discussions with the representatives of the National Association of Japanese Canadians at this moment. I know my honourable friend will be happy to learn that those negotiations are moving ahead and they are in the extremely capable hands of the Minister for Multiculturalism.

At that time, Gerry Weiner had not yet met again with the NAJC. Fearing that the government may be stalling until the House of Commons sessions closed, the NAJC informed the Minister that the Strategy Committee planned to fly to Ottawa in an attempt to meet with him. They would also call a press conference for August 24.

The trip to Ottawa was cancelled when Weiner finally made moves to negotiate a settlement with the NAJC.

NEGOTIATIONS IN MONTREAL

On August 18, 1988, Dennison Moore called Art Miki, saying that the government was eager to resolve redress directly with the NAJC. A secret meeting was set for August 25, in Montreal.

Arriving at the Ritz-Carlton Hotel, government officials swiftly ushered the NAJC Strategy Committee up a back staircase to the Chambre de Conseil. Present in the room were Gerry Weiner, Dennison Moore, Rick Clippendale, Alain Bisson from Department of Justice, Anne Scotton, a long-time worker in Multiculturalism who had been

Gerry Weiner, early in the second day of negotiations, August 25, 1988, with Dennison Moore, Chief of Staff, Alain Bisson, lawyer from the Department of Justice, and Maryka Omatsu. Photo: Cassandra Kobayashi.

135

(above) **Art Miki, Audrey Kobayashi, and Don Rosenbloom, NAJC legal advisor.**
Photo: Cassandra Kobayashi.

(above) **Roy Miki.**
Photo: Cassandra Kobayashi.

(above right) **Roy Miki and Maryka Omatsu.**
Photo: Cassandra Kobayashi.

involved in the early discussions under Jack Murta, and Lucien Bouchard, the Prime Minister's close friend, and Minister of State.

The presence of Bouchard was a surprise, but a sign that the government appeared ready to negotiate.

Bouchard opened with a startling change of position. The government was prepared to offer individual compensation, but the NAJC's figure of $25,000 was too high.

The negotiation process had finally begun.

Bouchard did not remain but said he was available, at any time, as each of the components of the NAJC's Redress Proposal was negotiated with the government's team.

Two days later, on August 27, 1988, after seventeen hours of negotiations, the NAJC and the government drafted the details of the Redress Agreement signed by the Prime Minister on September 22, 1988.

(above) **Anne Scotton and Rick Clippendale.** *Photo: Cassandra Kobayashi.*

(right) **Maryka Omatsu.** *Photo: Cassandra Kobayashi.*

(right) **The agreement was reached late in the evening of August 25, 1988.** *Photo: Cassandra Kobayashi.*

(top) **Cassandra Kobayashi and Art Miki.** *Photo: Roy Miki.*
(above) Photo: Cassandra Kobayashi.

137

(below, centre) **Seated: Gerry Weiner, Art Miki. Standing, left to right: Cassandra Kobayashi, Don Rosenbloom, Roger Obata, Rick Clippendale, Anne Scotton, Alain Bisson, Dennison Moore, Roy Miki, Maryka Omatsu, and Audrey Kobayashi.** *Courtesy of Cassandra Kobayashi.*

(below) **Gerry Weiner and Roger Obata, in the absence of Art Miki, signing the Redress Agreement on August 26, 1988.** *Photo: Cassandra Kobayashi.*

Art Miki in his hotel room just after reaching an agreement on August 25, 1988. *Photo: Cassandra Kobayashi.*

Terms of Agreement Between the Government of Canada and the National Association of Japanese Canadians

As a people, Canadians commit themselves to the creation of a society that ensures equality and justice for all, regardless of race or ethnic origin.

During and after World War II, Canadians of Japanese ancestry, the majority of whom were citizens, suffered unprecedented actions taken by the Government of Canada against their community.

Despite perceived military necessities at the time, the forced removal and internment of Japanese Canadians during World War II and their deportation and expulsion following the war, was unjust. In retrospect, government policies of disenfranchisement, detention, confiscation and sale of private and community property, expulsion, deportation and restriction of movement, which continued after the war, were influenced by discriminatory attitudes. Japanese Canadians who were interned had their property liquidated and the proceeds of sale were used to pay for their own internment.

The acknowledgement of these injustices serves notice to all Canadians that the excesses of the past are condemned and that the principles of justice and equality in Canada are reaffirmed.

Therefore, the Government of Canada, on behalf of all Canadians, does hereby:

1) acknowledge that the treatment of Japanese Canadians during and after World War II was unjust and violated principles of human rights as they are understood today;

2) pledge to ensure, to the full extent that its powers allow, that such events will not happen again; and

3) recognize, with great respect, the fortitude and determination of Japanese Canadians who, despite great stress and hardship, retain their commitment and loyalty to Canada and contribute so richly to the development of the Canadian nation.

As symbolic redress for those injustices, the Government offers:

a) $21,000 individual redress, subject to application by

Non-monetary Compensation

CITIZENSHIP

The settlement included a provision that those persons expelled by the Canadian government and their heirs could apply for Canadian citizenship in recognition that the exile of Canadians and landed immigrants was unjustified and served no military purpose. This offer was intended to provide an immigration route for those persons who would otherwise not meet all the usual Canadian immigration requirements.

CLEAR CONVICTION RECORDS

During and after World War II, some Japanese Canadians were convicted for infractions of orders in council passed under the War Measures Act that applied only to Japanese Canadians, such as the curfew, uprooting, and exclusion from the 100-mile coastal zone. The settlement agreement provided that the records of conviction would be cleared because it is now acknowledged by the government of Canada that the laws under which they were convicted were based on racism and therefore repugnant to the democratic principles Canada aspires to practice.

Some Japanese Canadians erroneously believed that they had a criminal record because they had been detained by the RCMP in the Immigration Hall in Vancouver, or put behind barbed wire in Petawawa or Angler, Ontario prisoner of war camps, for violation of curfew or failure to co-operate with the BC Security Commission. Because they were incarcerated without charges or trial, the settlement provision for the clearing of records does not apply to them because they technically had no record of conviction.

CANADIAN RACE RELATIONS FOUNDATION

It was always the NAJC's intention that the redress settlement contain elements to help prevent legalized racism. Towards that end, and as a gift to all Canadians, the NAJC agreed to contribute $12 million towards a national foundation for the elimination of racism in commemoration of those Japanese Canadians who suffered the injustices during and after World War II. The government of Canada contributed a matching $12 million.

---

eligible persons of Japanese ancestry who, during this period, were subjected to internment, relocation, deportation, loss of property or otherwise deprived of the full enjoyment of fundamental rights and freedoms based solely on the fact that they were of Japanese ancestry; each payment would be made in a tax-free lump sum, as expeditiously as possible;

b) $12 million to the Japanese-Canadian community, through the National Association of Japanese Canadians, to undertake educational, social and cultural activities or programmes that contribute to the well-being of the community or that promote human rights;

c) $12 million, on behalf of Japanese Canadians and in commemoration of those who suffered these injustices, and matched by a further $12 million from the Government of Canada, for the creation of a Canadian Race Relations Foundation that will foster racial harmony and cross-cultural understanding and help to eliminate racism;

d) subject to application by eligible persons, to clear the names of persons of Japanese ancestry who were convicted of violations under the War Measures Act or the National Emergency Transitional Powers Act;

e) subject to application by eligible persons, to grant Canadian citizenship to persons of Japanese ancestry still living who were expelled from Canada or had their citizenship revoked during the period 1941 to 1949, and to their living descendants;

f) to provide, through contractual arrangements, up to $3 million to the National Association of Japanese Canadians for their assistance, including community liaison, in administration of redress over the period of implementation.

Only persons alive at the date of the signing of these Terms of Agreement would be entitled to the redress in paragraphs (a), (d) and (e), except that the redress in (e) would also apply to descendants living at that date.

SETTLEMENT DAY,
September 22, 1988

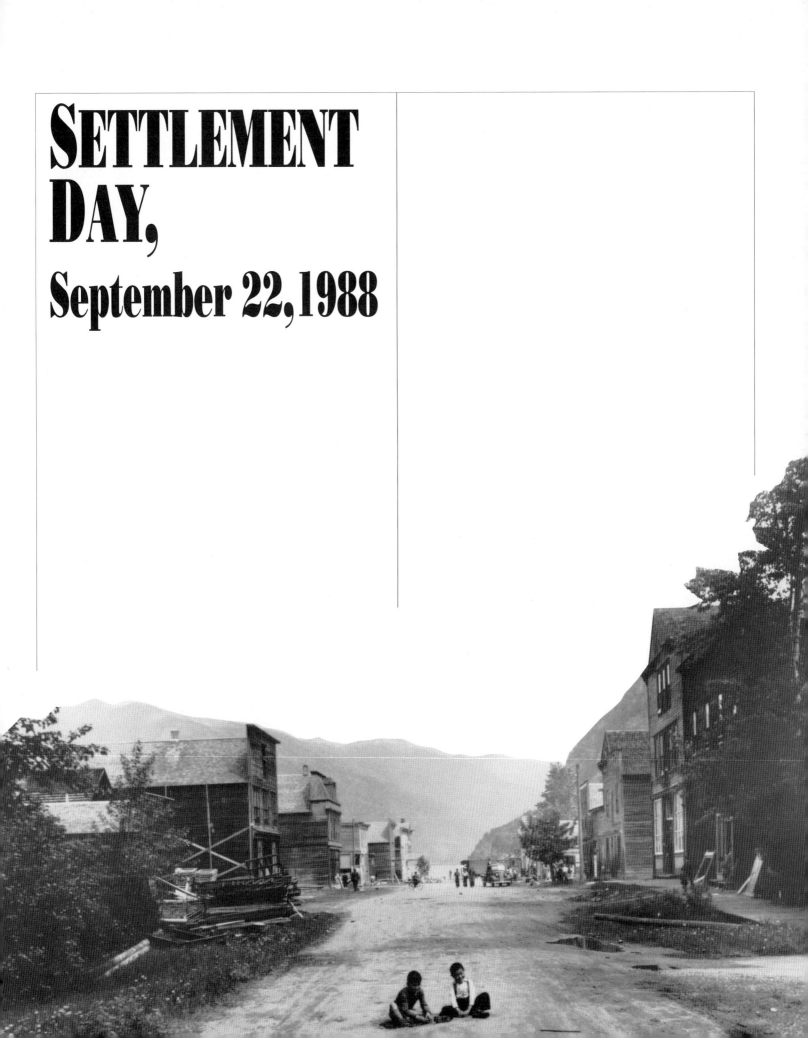

[Source for speeches by Brian Mulroney, Sergio Marchi, Ed Broadbent: Hansard, *House of Commons, September 22, 1988]*

PRIME MINISTER BRIAN MULRONEY IN THE HOUSE OF COMMONS:

Mr. Speaker, nearly half a century ago, in the crisis of wartime, the Government of Canada wrongfully incarcerated, seized the property, and disenfranchised thousands of citizens of Japanese ancestry. We cannot change the past. But we must, as a nation, have the courage to face up to these historical facts.

The issue of Japanese-Canadian redress is one which I raised in the House of Commons more than four years ago with the Prime Minister of the day when I was Leader of the Opposition. I said then in this House:

There is a world of difference between regret and a formal apology. Canadians of Japanese origin had their rights trampled upon. The reputation of this country was besmirched.

Since then, Mr. Speaker, the present Government has sought a settlement with the Japanese-Canadian community to put things right between them and their country; to put things right with the surviving members of the Japanese-Canadian wartime community of 22,000 persons; to put things right with their children, and ours, so that they can walk together in this country, burdened neither by the wrongs nor the grievances of previous generations.

It is fitting that representatives of the National Association of Japanese Canadians are present in the visitors' gallery on this solemn occasion because

(left) **Prime Minister Brian Mulroney and NAJC President Art Miki, immediately after signing the Redress Agreement, September 22, 1988.**
Photo: Gordon King.

today I have the honour to announce, on behalf of the Government of Canada, that a comprehensive redress settlement has been reached with the National Association of Japanese Canadians on behalf of their community.

Perhaps the most important element of this redress is the official acknowledgement of the wrongs of the 1940s. But redress must go beyond words and laws—important as they are for our present understanding and our future actions. The Minister of State for Multiculturalism and Citizenship (Mr. Weiner) will be announcing the details of the settlement, and I pay special tribute today to his skill and resolve in this matter, and to the Secretary of State (Mr. Bouchard) who, immediately after his swearing in as a Minister of the Crown, made the resolution of this important moral issue a matter of the highest priority for him and his colleagues. In a special way, I readily acknowledge the strong moral leadership on this particular question and, indeed, others, that has long been provided by the Honourable Member for Vancouver South (Mr. Fraser), the very distinguished Speaker of the House of Commons.

Mr. Speaker, I think all Members of the House know that no amount of money can right the wrong, undo the harm, and heal the wounds. But it is symbolic of our determination to address this issue, not only in the moral sense but also in a tangible way. In that spirit, we will accept applications for the granting of Canadian citizenship to eligible persons of Japanese ancestry who were expelled from Canada or had their citizenship revoked during these years. We will also accept requests for the clearing of names of eligible persons of Japanese ancestry who were convicted of violations under the War Measures Act—thankfully now gone from our texts of law in Canada—and the National Emergency Transitional Powers Act.

143

(below and right) **Japanese Canadians saying goodbye at the Slocan City train station, summer 1946. Some 4,000 were exiled to Japan** *after the war ended.* Photos: *Probably Tak Toyota, National Archives of Canada C47389, C47397.*

As well, in commemoration of all who suffered these injustices, we will establish a Canadian Race Relations Foundation to foster racial harmony and cross-cultural understanding in Canada.

Mr. Speaker, not only was the treatment inflicted on Japanese Canadians during the War both morally and legally unjustified, it went against the very nature of our country, of Canada. We are a pluralistic society. We each respect the language, opinions and religious convictions of our neighbour. We celebrate our linguistic duality and our cultural diversity. We know that the strength of our country lies in the collective energies of its regions. We are tolerant people who live in freedom in a land of abundance. That is the Canada of our ancestors. That is the Canada our ancestors worked to build. That is the kind of country we want to leave our children, the Canada of the Charter of Rights and Freedoms, the new Official Languages Act and the Canadian Multiculturalism Act. A Canada that at all times and in all circumstances works hard to eliminate racial discrimination at home and abroad.

A Canada, Mr. Speaker, that is able to face up to the mistakes of the past, and so become better prepared to face the challenges of the future.

I am tabling at this time the specific terms of the Government's historic agreement with the National Association of Japanese Canadians. I will meet later this morning with the President of the National Association of Japanese Canadians and some of his colleagues who are with him today to formalize this special agreement.

Most of us in our own lives have had occasion to regret certain things that we have done. Error is an ingredient of humanity, so too is apology and forgiveness. We all have learned from personal experience that as inadequate as apologies are they are the only way we can cleanse the past so that we may, as best we can, in good conscience face the future.

I know that I speak for Members on all sides of the House today in offering to Japanese Canadians the formal and sincere apology of this Parliament for those past injustices against them, against their families, and against their heritage, and our solemn commitment and undertaking to Canadians of every origin that such violations will never again in this country be countenanced or repeated.

SERGIO MARCHI (YORK WEST), FOR THE LIBERAL PARTY:

It is an honour for me to rise on behalf of my colleagues in the Liberal Party caucus in response to the very historic announcement made only moments ago by the Right Honourable Prime Minister (Mr. Mulroney). My Leader finds himself in Vancouver this morning and, unfortunately, will not be in a position to respond in kind on the floor of the House of Commons. However, he will be making a statement from Vancouver on this very historic announcement later in the day.

> *"All I want is the satisfaction from the government that we won our case. I lost the most productive years of my life. I was just existing to keep the wolves from the door."*
>
> *Tad Wakabayashi, from "The Wound That Hasn't Healed," by Tim Harper,* Toronto Star, *February 22, 1987.*

As the Prime Minister indicated, the Minister of State for Multiculturalism and Citizenship (Mr. Weiner) will be revealing the details of the redress package later today. I have yet to see those details, but I trust that they will be in keeping with the aspirations articulated so well for so long by the National Association of Japanese Canadians, and agreeable to the Japanese Canadians citizens and residents in that very proud community.

Towards that end, I am pleased today that the federal Government and this Parliament has moved to redress the injustices that were inflicted against an important and integral part of our Canadian society, Canadian citizens who happened to be of Japanese ancestry. In doing so, it closes the chapter of what was a very sad and sensitive memory in our history.

While one's home, land, and business once lost

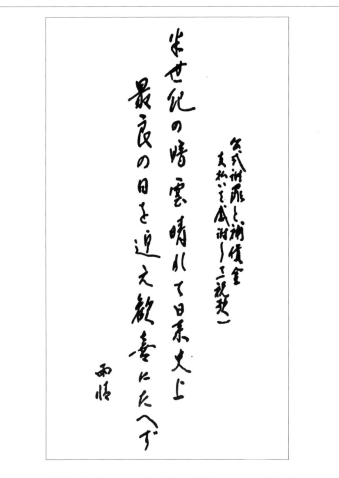

Kooshiki Shadai to Hoshookin Shihara o Kansha shite Oiwai no Uta

Hanseiki no
Anun harete
Nikkei shijyo
Sairyo no hi o mukae
Kanki ni taezu.

A Commemorative Poem of Thanks for the Public Apology and Payment of Compensation Funds

Our dark cloud of a half century dissipated,
The fairest day
In Japanese-Canadian history
Dawns.
Our joy is unsurpassable.

Tanka by Takeo Ujo Nakano
Translated by Leatrice Nakano Willson

(right and below) ***Slocan City, 1942, one of various abandoned towns—so-called "ghost towns"—that was repaired for use as a detention centre for Japanese Canadians who were uprooted from the west coast.*** *Photo: National Archives of Canada C137795, C137788, C137792.*

can never be replaced, and while being evicted from one's own community and separated from one's own family and friends leaves a deep and emotional scar that can never be completely erased from the soul of those Canadian citizens, today's commitment by Government and by Parliament will serve as best as possible to heal those very deep wounds and concerns.

Moreover, today's actions are underlined by an important and symbolic message, a message of fairness and justice for all, that this nation stands for equality for all Canadians, and that there can only be, and must only be, one first-class citizenship for all Canadians.

It is with a great sense of pride and history, therefore, that I am able to speak on behalf of my Party and join the Prime Minister in issuing this most important apology to the Japanese Canadian community of Canada.

It is not a sign of weakness for a country to render this apology. Instead, it is a sure sign of strength and a sign of reflection of our country's commitment to try wherever and however to right our wrongs, not merely for the sake of correcting the history books but, more important perhaps, to establish important standards that will serve Canadians today and future generations of Canadians tomorrow. In addition, today's actions are not so much about a multicultural issue as much as about an issue of Canadian justice.

In closing, I wish to pay a special tribute and commend Mr. Art Miki, his colleagues from the National Association of Japanese Canadians, and its members and friends in the Japanese Canadian community at large, for their never ending determination and deep belief in the cause that they carried so well for so long. Today's resolution, no doubt, is a tribute to their sense of purpose, but it is also an appropriate response to those who continue to question the legitmacy and motivation of the leadership of the National Association of Japanese Canadians.

It is also fitting that the Prime Minister pointed out the pivotal role played behind the scenes by our Honourable Speaker who, I can say publicly to him, offered us a sense of encouragement in the day-to-day questions that we posed on the floor of the House of Commons over the last four years. I join in saluting our Honourable Speaker, and indeed the other Members of Parliament who may not be making a statement this morning but who nevertheless played a significant role.

Finally, on this historic day, we cannot forget the many Japanese Canadians who were interned but who are no longer with us, unfortunately. Their children refuse to forget the hardship of their forefathers. It would have been my hope, indeed it would have been our collective hope, that they too could be with us today to witness and be part of the day that they had dearly longed for.

However, I say today, and I believe all Members share this, that their struggles were not in vain for their efforts kept that flame of hope alive and bright. It was the strength of that flame that provided the foundation for today's resolution. This agreement, in large part, is their agreement as well.

EDWARD BROADBENT (OSHAWA), LEADER OF THE NEW DEMOCRATIC PARTY:

Mr. Speaker, I listened with great pleasure to the Prime Minister's speech today. Forty-six years ago, the Government of Canada took measures against Japanese Canadians that were unjust and unacceptable. Today, at last, we have started to make amends.

In the 1940s our Government, a democratically elected Government, did a great injustice to some

On the Occasion of Our Redress Celebration

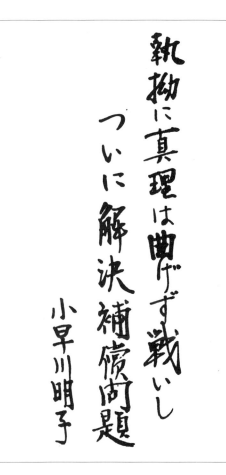

Shitsuyo ni
Shinri wa magezu
Tatakaishi
Tsuini kaiketsu
Hosho mondai

Reaching for justice
In time's persistence,
Unwaveringly
At last—
Our redress resolution.

Tanka by Haruko Kobayakawa

22,000 of our citizens, a permanent injustice to those who are no longer living. This was done, not because of what they had done, but because of who they were. These Japanese Canadians had their families broken up, their property confiscated, their businesses destroyed. They were forced to abandon their homes on the coast of British Columbia and they were forced to move to the interior and to elsewhere in Canada.

They, as Canadian citizens, had done no wrong. They were the victims of intolerance and racism brought about, not because we were at war with them but because we were at war with the land of their ancestors. They had done no wrong to any of their fellow citizens. It was an inglorious moment in our, on the whole, proud history.

Today we are formally acknowledging this wrong, and I am pleased that today's representatives of Canadians of Japanese ancestry have been able to reach an agreement with the Government of Canada. On behalf of all members of my Party and, I am sure in a sense I speak for everyone in the House of Commons and Canadians wherever they may live, I bid a special welcome to those Canadians of Japanese ancestry who are with us today in the House of Commons.

I would like to stress that when we talk about the grievous injustice that was inflicted, we are not talking about an abstract breaking of an abstract right. We are talking about profound, serious human suffering. As an example, I would like to cite a quotation from an extremely moving Canadian novel by a Canadian of Japanese ancestry. It is called

> *" I think all ethnic groups should be pleased that finally a wrong has been corrected."*
>
> *Yaroslaw Kulba, President, Montreal branch of Ukrainian Canadian Committee; quoted in "Montreal's Japanese Celebrate Settlement," by Debbie Parkes, Montreal Gazette, September 24, 1988.*

Obasan, and it is written by Joy Kogawa. It is a story of the life experience of families at this time. It is noted that the families are fictional but all experiences are very real. At one point the heroine of the novel, who is in her thirties, describes the impact this had on her life. She says:

> The fact is I never got used to it and I cannot, I cannot bear the memory. There are some nightmares from which there is no waking, only deeper and deeper sleep.
>
> There is a word for it. Hardship. The hardship is so pervasive, so inescapable, so thorough it's a noose around my chest and I cannot move anymore. (*Obasan* [Penguin, 1983], p. 194)

I repeat, Mr. Speaker, these have been real experiences in real lives for which our parliamentary ancestors have to assume responsibility because they made those decisions that led to that experience. As the Prime Minister (Mr. Mulroney) has said, we all make errors. Our predecessors in this great Chamber of ours made errors. One of the important and fundamental ways of addressing these errors is at least to apologize publicly and acknowledge the serious wrong that was done, and that we are doing. However, in so doing, we must keep in mind that it does not mitigate at all the horrible experience that has been inflicted upon those victims.

The Prime Minister quite appropriately alluded to the work that has been done by present generations in redressing this wrong here in the House. I think it might have been appropriate to cite those people who stood up at the time because they were present. They were Canadians who said it was wrong, who went against the force of public opinion, who fought for civil liberties at a time when it was important to do the fighting and not talk about redressing wrongs that were done by others. It is easy for us in one sense, although appropriate, to do that. I would like to cite a few words of a distinguished Member of Parliament at that time. He had this to say, clearly in the face of public opinion:

If we are to have harmonious and friendly relations between the oriental population and the rest of our British Columbia citizens, we must stop discriminating against and abusing the orientals. We must find some common ground on which we can work, and I think it can be found...I am satisfied that if we treat the Japanese and our other oriental citizens right, we shall get their loyalty...

He went on to say:

I know them, speak to them; I visit them and have them in my home, and I have not the slightest doubt that what I say is correct. If we are to avoid the troubles that other countries have had with racial minorities, then we must take a realistic view of the situation in British Columbia and attempt to make these people feel at home among us. We will secure their loyalty by fairness and kindness and by the practice of those other attributes which we exercise in our relations with other people.

He was speaking to fellow Canadian citizens. That speech was given in this House on February 25, 1941, by Angus MacInnis, the then Member for Vancouver-Kingsway.

I want simply to conclude by complimenting the Government of the day on behalf of my Party in reaching this agreement and by saying, as one politician: I hope this kind of experience for us as a nation will never ever be repeated.

(top) *Joy Kogawa with Ed Broadbent at the reception in the Parliament Building immediately after the signing of the Redress Agreement, September 22, 1988.* Photo: Gordon King.

(above) *Mas Takahashi and Amy Yamazaki, both from Ottawa, with John Fraser, Speaker of the House, at the reception following the signing of the Redress Agreement.*
Photo: Gordon King.

149

GERRY WEINER, Minister of State for Multiculturalism, from his Press Statement:

Ladies and gentlemen, for over forty years successive Canadian Governments have refused to acknowledge or to redress the shameful injustices done to Japanese Canadians during the Second World War and after.

Of approximately 22,000 Japanese Canadians who were uprooted, relocated, interned or deported during this time, the vast majority were Canadian citizens. And let me emphasize—most were born here in Canada.

The Prime Minister pledged in 1984 that his Government would do everything possible to right the wrongs of the past as best we can today. This was not an easy pledge to fulfill. The issues are complex and determining appropriate redress for the loss of dignity, of honour and self-pride, of basic human rights is extremely difficult.

It is therefore with deep feelings of humility and pride that I share with you details of an agreement on Japanese Canadian redress, announced by the Prime Minister in the House of Commons today.

This is an historic agreement. And it is an honourable and meaningful settlement.

But before going into details let me tell you about the principles which guided and defined our negotiations.

First, we sought to reach an agreement that would have the support of the National Association of Japanese Canadians (NAJC), on behalf of the Japanese Canadian community.

Second, we wanted to ensure that this kind of injustice could *never happen again* in this country.

And third, we struggled to finalize an agreement now for compassionate reasons. We were mindful of those Japanese Canadians whose health or advancing age might deprive them of knowing that the shame on their honour, their dignity, their rights as Canadians is now removed forever.

Let me remind you that these people were stripped of their fundamental rights and freedoms.

Their entire community was torn apart. Their land, their homes, their personal property were taken from them. Family members were cruelly separated from each other. And *none* of these persons was ever charged with any act of sabotage or disloyalty.

Why *did* they remain loyal to this country?

Only someone who is Japanese Canadian can explain. So let me share with you the words of Joy Kogawa from her award-winning book *Obasan*. Here Kogawa is describing why her Aunt Emily, a "nisei" or second-generation Japanese Canadian, fought for acknowledgement of the injustice done to her people.

When war struck this country, when neither pride nor belligerence nor grief had availed us anything, when we were uprooted, and scattered to the four winds, I clung desperately to those immortal lines:

This *is* my own, *my* native land.

Later still, after our former homes had been sold over our vigorous protests, after having been re-registered, finger-printed, card-indexed, roped and restricted, I cry out the question:

Is this my own, my native land?

The answer cannot be changed. Yes. It is. For better or worse, *I am Canadian*. (*Obasan* [Penguin, 1983], p. 140)

The key to our negotiations really lies in that final sentence. The Canadian Government of the time committed unfair, discriminatory acts against loyal

(left) **NAJC President Art Miki with Gerry Weiner, Minister of State for Multiculturalism.** *Photo: Gordon King.*

(below) **Lewis Chan, President of the Canadian Ethnocultural Council, speaking at the NAJC press conference, September 22, 1988.** *Photo: Cassandra Kobayashi.*

Canadians. This Government is now acknowledging those wrongs and promising that they *must never happen again*.

...In addition, we have replaced the War Measures Act with the new Emergencies Act. This was one of the settlement measures sought by the NAJC, and I would like to point out that this new Act equips the Government to provide for the safety and security of Canadians while limiting exceptional measures to no more than is absolutely needed.

I believe that all these measures demonstrate how much Canada has matured in forty years. The Canadian Human Rights Act...the Canadian Charter of Rights and Freedoms...the Canadian Multiculturalism Act which became law in July...And now this historic Japanese Canadian Redress Agreement...These and other initiatives will help counter discrimination and injustice wherever and whenever they are found.

And they demonstrate clearly that we are a nation capable of learning from the sometimes bitter mistakes of the past to build an even better future for us all.

We *are* prepared to confront prejudice or discrimination or racism—and call them unacceptable.

Our society of today would *not* tolerate what took place forty years ago. We, as Canadians, have indeed changed and grown. We have acquired new wisdom and compassion. And, over the years, we have recognized the reality and the vast potential of our multicultural identity.

This Government's official acknowledgement of the injustices done to Japanese Canadians serves notice to all Canadians that the excesses of the past are condemned and that the principles of justice and equality in Canada are reaffirmed.

I want to say how much I am looking forward to a close partnership with Mr. Miki and other representatives of the National Association of Japanese Canadians as we begin to implement the terms of the settlement.

Working together, we can say *never again* with genuine conviction and understanding. We *can* continue to build a better and fairer society for all Canadians. And, believe me, we will.

151

ART MIKI, PRESS CONFERENCE, SEPTEMBER 22, 1988:

Today is the day we celebrate justice and human rights in Canada. It is an historic day for Canadians of Japanese ancestry who have been struggling so long to resolve the injustices of the 1940s.

What does the settlement mean? First, it means that the importance of the process of negotiations that we had stressed with the government was achieved through our negotiations with Honourable Gerry Weiner. For Canadians of Japanese ancestry, this settlement means that there is now an official acknowledgement which the Prime Minister announced today in the House of Commons, an official recognition that there were grave injustices inflicted upon its citizens by the government of that day. Through the settlement the burden of guilt that many had carried for years was lifted. I recall the words of David Suzuki at the Ottawa Redress Forum where he expressed regret that his mother died as an

"enemy alien" without ever hearing the government's apology and acknowledgement for the wrong. Many in our community will feel satisfied that the government finally absolved them from any wrong and now can continue their lives as true Canadians.

For all Canadians the Redress Settlement is a demonstration by the government of a strong commitment towards the preservation of human rights and justice, and the protection of minority rights. This adds to the strengthening of the Charter of Rights and Freedoms, the Multiculturalism Act, and the Canadian Constitution. This settlement is a landmark for human rights. That is the reason why we pursued redress.

The other question that has been raised is "why today?" Although it has taken four and a half years, I always felt that there would be a time and place when things would happen and that you wait for that time. We waited patiently. We worked on this together with the hope that someday there would be this time and place. Why today? The media must be congratulated because they educated the Canadian public on the Japanese Canadian experience and the purpose for redress. I can recall as I flew across Canada the many people I encountered who had very little or no knowledge of the injustices suffered by Japanese Canadians during and after the war. We have a different picture today. The understanding and knowledge of Canadians have increased greatly and we don't have to be ashamed or apologize for seeking redress.

The signing of the American redress bill in August 1988 gave us hope and an incentive to carry on our mission. Furthermore, by July and August 1988 there was a willingness by the Minister and Prime Minister to tackle the issue head on and not to try to divert us in some other direction. Finally, the possibility of the upcoming election may have had some influence.

Through the redress struggle, there were many who contributed, not only in assisting us in Ottawa but also providing support during the difficult times. As I mentioned previously, the media strengthened our community because each time the redress issue was voiced publicly, strong support through their coverage and editorials increased our credibility. The politicians, Sergio Marchi and Ernie Epp, who is not present today, were strong advocates in the House and enlisted the support of their leaders, John Turner and Ed Broadbent. The role of John Fraser was mentioned by the Prime Minister today. In our meetings with him, Mr. Fraser gave us moral support to carry on. We appeared before the Standing Committee on Multiculturalism several times. They listened to our concerns and saw the need to see the issue resolved. The Canadian Ethnocultural Council, Lewis Chan, President, and Andrew Cardozo who are here, and others, met with the Prime Minister to discuss the redress issue. The National Coalition for Japanese Canadian Redress made up of ethnic

(left) **David Murata at Sutton Place Hotel where Japanese Canadians in Toronto gathered to celebrate the signing of the Redress Agreement, September 22, 1988. He was the NAJC's co-ordinator for the Redress Rally in Ottawa, April 14, 1988.** *Photo: Cassandra Kobayashi.*

(above) **Prime Minister Brian Mulroney, after signing the Redress Agreement in the Parliament Building, personally congratulated NAJC President Art Miki for his work in achieving the Redress Settlement.** *Photo: Gordon King.*

(opposite page) **Japanese Canadians being exiled to Japan, at the train station, Slocan City, BC, summer 1946.** *Photo: Tak Toyota, National Library of Canada C46350.*

organizations, union, church, and civil liberties groups all over the country helped push the redress movement forward. As you can see there was very much support within our country.

The new Emergencies Act was passed earlier. One of our goals was to ensure that other groups would be protected from future injustices. Although there are some areas in the new Act that need to be strengthened, we feel that this is a positive step and I hope we as an organization will continue to work with the government to make the Act even stronger. It may never be perfect but we must continue to monitor and work towards improving it.

We are very pleased with the settlement. I feel that all of the components in our proposal of 1986 have been addressed. We were pleased to contribute $12 million with an equal contribution from the government to create a foundation to fight racism. This is extremely important to all the communities. We found that in our struggle for redress we needed assistance. We hope that this foundation will provide

the type of assistance we found difficult to get. I know for many of us this is not the end. People have said to me, "I guess you're relieved that it's all over." I must say that with the responsibilities bestowed upon us by the government, it is just the beginning because there is much work to be done in rebuilding the Japanese Canadian community. I know that our communities are looking forward to this challenge.

I do appreciate the support that has been expressed through the media and the faith that has been shown by Canadians, because this is a great day. I don't know how else to express my feelings but to jump up, shout and yell, which I won't do, but that's the kind of feeling I have. I'm very proud to be here today, and very proud to be a Canadian.

The PNE Plaque: The Scene Behind the Scene

(left) **Bunk beds at Hastings Park where many Japanese Canadians were confined before they were sent away from the west coast.**
Photo: Vancouver Public Library #14917.

On April 1, 1989, a federal government plaque from the Historic Sites and Monuments Board commemorating the internment of Japanese Canadians, was unveiled and then placed at the entrance to Hastings Park, now known as the Pacific National Exhibition (PNE) grounds. It was here that some 8,000 uprooted Japanese Canadians were confined before being shipped inland from the coast. The site is a painful reminder of the degrading living conditions many had to endure, especially the women and children, who were placed in former livestock barns.

No one questioned the appropriateness of the plaque on that day, six months after the Redress Settlement, but the event had had a stormy history. During 1987, the Greater Vancouver Japanese Canadian Citizens' Association (JCCA) got embroiled in a battle with the PNE Board, chaired by Irwin Swanguard, after the board rejected the federal government's plaque proposal. Some directors did not want the public to know about the PNE's wartime use, and others even argued that the uprooting was justified as a security measure. For the local Japanese Canadians who had been confined in the park, these attitudes were reminiscent of the racism prevalent in the 1940s. After a lengthy period of organized protest, the Vancouver JCCA made a successful appeal to Vancouver City Council—and a decision was made to install the plaque at the entrance to the park, on land beyond the jurisdiction of the PNE Board.

Japanese Canadians were fighting for more than just a monument. They were calling for a public acknowledgement of injustices which would help set the historical record straight, and to educate Canadians. So it was that this local controversy, coming at the end of the long struggle by Canadian citizens of Japanese ancestry for public recognition of their rights, mirrored the larger national redress struggle in miniature.

> *"In achieving this redress settlement, the NAJC pays tribute to all Canadians who shared the Japanese Canadian dream of justice in our time. Over the past five years, the internment story has been kept alive by informed and attentive reporters from all media, and editorials from major newspapers have commented thoughtfully on the crucial developments in the NAJC's campaign for a just and honourable settlement. The victory for justice and human rights is also a victory for the democratic process."*
>
> *From the NAJC Press Release, September 22, 1988.*

National Association of Japanese Canadians
National Council, May 1986 to October 1988

EXECUTIVE COMMITTEE:
Art Miki, *President*
Roger Obata, *Vice-President*
Harold Hirose, *Treasurer*

PRESIDENT'S COMMITTEE:
Fred Kaita
Henry Kojima
Carol Matsumoto
Lil Mukai
Joy Ooto
Lucy Yamashita
Alan Yoshino

STRATEGY COMMITTEE:
Art Miki
Roger Obata
Roy Inouye
Bryce Kanbara
Audrey Kobayashi
Cassandra Kobayashi
Roy Miki
Maryka Omatsu

LEGAL ADVISORS:
Shin Imai
Cassandra Kobayashi
Maryka Omatsu
Don Rosenbloom
Ann Sunahara

The following delegates and alternates attended meetings from May 1986 to October 1, 1988.

CALGARY:
Mas Kawanami
Jack Omura
Jim Tateishi

EDMONTON:
Gordon Hirabayashi
Allan Hoyano
George Tsuruda

HAMILTON:
Bryce Kanbara
Eugene Maikawa
Norm Oikawa
Tim Oikawa

KAMLOOPS:
Betty Inouye
Roy Inouye
George Nishimura

KELOWNA:
George Kakuno
Fumi Ono

LETHBRIDGE:
Jerry Hisaoka
Tom Mitsunaga
Mas Terakita

MANITOBA:
Terumi Kuwada
Carol Matsumoto
Keiko Miki
Theresa Oye
Howard Omoto
Jim Suzuki
Caroline Yamashita

OTTAWA:
Elmer Hara
Sachiko Okuda
Mas Takahashi
Aki Watanabe

THUNDER BAY:
Jim Inaba
Ken Taniwa

TORONTO:
Charlotte Chiba
Wes Fujiwara
Van Hori
Ken Kishibe
Joy Kogawa
Bill Kobayashi
Maryka Omatsu
Emmy Nakay
Ken Noma
Roger Obata

QUEBEC:
Kathleen Hayami
Audrey Kobayashi

VANCOUVER:
Tatsuo Kage
Gordon Kayahara
Cassandra Kobayashi
Roy Miki
Irene Nemeth
Ken Shikaze
Dan Tokawa

VANCOUVER ISLAND:
Gordon Kayahara
Masako Fukawa
Les Kojima
Dick Nakamura

VERNON:
Tosh Yakura

ACKNOWLEDGEMENTS

Early in 1988, during the final phase of the NAJC's redress movement, an educational pamphlet was hastily written and produced in Vancouver by the Greater Vancouver Japanese Canadian Citizens' Association (JCCA) Redress Committee. Called *Justice in Our Time: Redress for Japanese Canadians*, this 16-page publication was timed for distribution at a series of redress rallies organized in NAJC centres across Canada, which culminated in the large Ottawa Rally on April 14, 1988. The National Coalition for Japanese Canadian Redress, a broad-based group of prominent individuals and organizations formed in the fall of 1987, was growing rapidly in the early months of 1988, and members' names were listed in the pamphlet to encourage other Canadians to join in the NAJC's call for a negotiated redress settlement.

Although this *Justice in Our Time* bears few traces of the earlier pamphlet, the title itself has been retained. Thirty months after the historic settlement, the dream of "justice in our time" has remained the most compelling force behind the long years of struggle. Today, this phrase captures the significance of Japanese Canadian redress as a celebration and affirmation of human rights.

•

Diane Kadota and Mary Schendlinger deserve special acknowledgement for their dedicated and valuable work on the pamphlet *Justice in Our Time* (NAJC, 1988).

The work of gathering photos and documents to accompany the text was made all the more rewarding because of the generosity—and in many cases, the hospitality—of those individuals who allowed us to reproduce material from their family archives. Many others responded to our irritating requests for assistance, often taking time off from a busy schedule to help us locate some required information. Our sincere thanks to Yosh Arai, Phillip Doi, Ben Fiber, Wes and Misao Fujiwara, Jennifer Hashimoto, Susan (Kobayashi) Hidaka, Harold Hirose, Nancy Hoita, Van Hori, Shin Imai, Lucy Ishii, Gordon Kadota, Connie Kadota, Fred Kambayashi, Bryce Kanbara, Tameo and Fumiko (Shimoda) Kanbara, Roy Kawamoto, Yone and Coby Kobayashi, Ken Kishibe, Amy Kuwabara, Terumi Kuwada, Nobuko (Wani) Matsui, Roy Matsui, Art Miki, Shizuko Miki, Waylen Miki, Rei Nakashima, Tak Nishino, Roger Obata, Tom Oikawa, Irene Oizumi, Don Sato, Kyoshi Shimizu, Irene (Kato) Tsuyuki, and Harry Yonekura.

Many organizations assisted with photos and research materials: the staff of the NAJC office in Winnipeg, the Greater Vancouver Japanese Canadian Citizens' Association (JCCA) and the former Vancouver JCCA Redress Committee, the Japanese Canadian Centennial Project (JCCP) Redress Committee, *Nikkei Voice*, the Toronto Chapter of the NAJC, the Japanese American Citizens League, the Richmond Public Archives, Special Collections at the University of British Columbia, the Vancouver *Sun*, the Vancouver Public Library, the United States Library of Congress, the National Archives of Canada and the National Library of Canada, the Japanese Canadian Secretariat in Ottawa, especially former Director Anne Scotton, June Takahashi, and Roy Kawamoto, and the Japanese Canadian Cultural Centre in Toronto, especially Sam Ariza and Kunio Suiyama.

We are grateful to photographer Manon Lessard for her excellent work in preparing the photographs for reproduction; to Margaret Wheat Prior, Geography Department, Simon Fraser University, for making the maps; to the Estate of Haruko Kobayakawa and Ujo Nakano for permission to reproduce their poems; to Betty Toyota for permission to reproduce photos by Tak Toyota in the National Library; to Tatsuo Kage for advice on Japanese words and terms; to photographers John Flanders and Tamio Wakayama for permission to use their photos; to Roy Peterson for permission to reproduce his cartoon from the Vancouver *Sun*; and to Adèle Tremblay for assistance in translating Gilles Tardif's speech in French.

Special appreciation to Gordon King for volunteering to be the NAJC photographer at the Ottawa Rally and on the day of the redress settlement, and to Tony Tamayose for his enthusiastic support and his assistance on many production tasks.

Ann Sunahara offered useful advice and additional information for the historical section, and Karl Siegler at Talonbooks gave valuable editorial assistance throughout the preparation of the manuscript.

Our heartfelt thanks to Slavia Miki for her patience, encouragement, feedback, record-keeping, and personal support for this project, from beginning to end.

•

Our own involvement in the NAJC's redress movement, at the local level in Vancouver and at the national level with the NAJC Council, was all-consuming from 1984 to 1988. As members of the NAJC Strategy Committee, we were also able to participate directly in the educational and political work that led to the negotiated settlement.

We are grateful to the NAJC Council for giving us the opportunity to write this account of the redress movement. As far as possible, we have attempted to document the chronology of events as they unfolded through the perspective of the NAJC. Given the highly complicated and multi-dimensional nature of redress, there will no doubt be other accounts written. We hope that the story presented here will "ring true" for those Japanese Canadians who took an active part in the redress movement, many of whose comments during the years of the campaign, in print or in conversation, helped to shape our understanding of redress. This has been our intention—but, of course, we assume responsibility for the research materials chosen, for factual accuracy, and for the overall interpretation of the redress movement.

Roy Miki
Cassandra Kobayashi
May 8, 1991
Vancouver, BC

BIBLIOGRAPHY OF WORKS CITED

Books, pamphlets, and government documents cited are listed in this bibliography. Bibliographic data for newspaper articles and government documents is included in the body of the text. Quoted material without bibliographic data is taken from the papers of the National Association of Japanese Canadians (NAJC).

Adachi, Ken. *The Enemy That Never Was.* Toronto: McClelland and Stewart, 1987; revised edition, 1991.

Berger, Tom. *Reflections on Redress.* Vancouver: Vancouver JCCA Redress Committee, 1986.

Commission on Wartime Relocation and Internment of Civilians. *Personal Justice Denied.* Report of the Commission on Wartime Relocation and Internment of Civilians. Washington, DC, December 1982.

House of Commons (Ottawa). *Debates,* August 4, 1944.

_____. *Equality Now!* Participation of Visible Minorities in Canadian Society. Ottawa: Queen's Printer, 1984.

_____. *Minutes of the Proceedings and Evidence of the Special Joint Committee of the Senate and of the House of Commons on the Constitution of Canada,* Wednesday, November 26, 1980.

Irons, Peter. *Justice at War: The Story of the Japanese American Internment Cases.* New York: Oxford University Press, 1983.

Ito, Roy. *We Went to War: The Story of the Japanese Canadians Who Served During the First and Second World Wars.* Stittsville, Ontario: Canada's Wings, 1984.

Japanese American Citizens League. *Coming Home.* Seattle: JACL, 1988.

Japanese Canadian Centennial Project (JCCP). *A Dream of Riches: The Japanese Canadians, 1877-1977.* Vancouver: JCCP, 1978.

Kogawa, Joy. *Obasan.* Markham, Ontario: Penguin Books, 1983.

Kobayashi, Audrey. *A Demographic Profile of Japanese Canadians and Social Implications for the Future.* Ottawa: Department of the Secretary of State, 1989.

Kobayashi, Cassandra and Roy Miki, eds. *Spirit of Redress: Japanese Canadians in Conference.* Vancouver: JC Publications, 1989.

Kitagawa, Muriel. *This Is My Own: Letters to Wes and Other Writings on Japanese Canadians 1941-1949.* Ed. Roy Miki. Vancouver: Talonbooks, 1985.

Miki, Roy. "The Experience of Racism." *Taking Stock.* Vancouver: British Columbia Organization to Fight Racism, 1986.

National Association of Japanese Canadians (NAJC). *Democracy Betrayed: The Case for Redress.* Winnipeg: NAJC, 1984.

_____. *The Case for Redress: Information.* Winnipeg: NAJC, 1984.

_____. *Economic Losses of Japanese Canadians After 1941: A Study Conducted by Price Waterhouse, Vancouver, BC.* Winnipeg: NAJC, 1985.

_____. *Justice in Our Time: Redress for Japanese Canadians.* Winnipeg: NAJC, 1988.

Redress for Japanese Canadians: A Community Forum. Ed. Roy Miki. Speeches by Joy Kogawa, Tom Shoyama, Ann Sunahara, and David Suzuki. Vancouver: JCCA Redress Committee, 1984.

Robertson, Heather. *Sugar Farmers of Manitoba.* Manitoba: The Manitoba Beet Growers Association, 1968.

Sunahara, Ann Gomer. *The Politics of Racism: The Uprooting of Japanese Canadians during the Second World War.* Toronto: Lorimer, 1981.

Tateishi, John. *And Justice for All: An Oral History of the Japanese American Detention Camps.* New York: Random House, 1984.

Tribune Juive. Les Canadiens d'origine japonaise/The Japanese Canadians. Montreal, Juillet-Aout, 1987.